My Family · My Friends My Food

RECIPES CELEBRATING PEOPLE AND LIFE

My Family · My Friends My Food

RECIPES CELEBRATING PEOPLE AND LIFE

Michael H. Flores

with foreword by
Susan Spicer

My Family · My Friends · My Food

RECIPES CELEBRATING PEOPLE AND LIFE

Published by Mis En Place, L.L.C.

Library of Congress Number: 2003094996
ISBN: 0-9740563-0-8

Edited and Manufactured by
Favorite Recipes® Press
An imprint of

FRP™

P.O. Box 305142
Nashville, TN 37230
800-358-0560

Cover and Chapter Opener Art: Brother Cletus Behlman, S.M.
Art Direction: Steve Newman
Book Design: Brad Whitfield
Project Editor: Georgia Brazil

Manufactured in the United States of America
First Printing 2003
6,000 copies

This Book is Dedicated to...

My Parents

Apolonio & Mary Helen

I am forever grateful for all you have given me and for the opportunities you have made possible. My dreams have become a reality because of you. You've always encouraged me to reach for the stars, often allowing me to stand on your shoulders to do so. Thank you.

And to My Brother

Tommy

My number one fan! Your smiles, laughs, and hugs are an inspiration. I will always take care of you; "I will never lose you."

I do love you!

Table of Contents

For Starters

Salads · Soups

Pasta

On the Side

Foreword

I first met Michael and his family when they came to dine at Bayona, my restaurant in New Orleans, many years ago. He was preparing to study at the Culinary Institute of America in New York. Not until it was time for Michael to do his externship for school did I hear from him again; he called and expressed an interest in working at Bayona and learning from me. As his parents were close friends of my partners, I agreed to accept him.

When Michael arrived in my kitchen, he brought some newfound skills and boundless enthusiasm for the foods he was preparing. It was because of this enthusiasm that I rotated him to various jobs throughout the kitchen. Some days he was the prep-cook, other days he was in charge of garde manger; he sweated on the hot line and made bread and desserts in the bakery. Michael learned the ropes at Bayona and became an integral part of the restaurant—like all of the staff. His appreciation and passion for putting flavors together impressed me tremendously—not to mention his tamale-making ability! I know Michael was sad when his externship with me was over. I told him that he was more than welcome to stay. He, however, said that it would probably be best if he returned to the Culinary Institute and finished his education. Although Michael seemed to enjoy the restaurant atmosphere, I was not surprised when I heard he had expanded his culinary horizons. I've seen him not only open a cooking school and kitchen store, but also develop his own gourmet product line. It's in this growing line of delicious and creative prepared foods that Michael seems to have found his true calling.

Michael is an active and caring member of his food community and has managed to make me a part of it. He has lured me to his hometown of San Antonio, Texas, from year to year to participate in numerous charity events. He's even charmed me into cooking in his family's home for the celebration of his parents' 25th wedding anniversary. It has been on these visits with Michael that I have had the chance to witness and taste his culinary progress. Building on a family tradition of Mexican and Texan specialties, he has found ways to blend some new and exciting ingredients with the classic staples of traditional fare. Now he has decided to share some of his secrets in this new book *My Family, My Friends, My Food: Recipes Celebrating People and Life*.

I am aware that in our hectic lives we do not have much time to spend in our kitchens. Michael knows how to communicate his ideas about food, and with this book as a guide, you will be able to make such divine, but earthly dishes as Salmon Salpicon or Grilled Cilantro Sweetbreads with a minimum of ingredients and complicated techniques. It's all about taste and not hours of slicing and dicing.

It has been a pleasure knowing Michael and experiencing bits and pieces of his world. I am excited for him and his first (and undoubtedly not last) cookbook. Somehow, I always knew he'd have one [cookbook] before I did. I look forward to stealing some of his recipes! Enjoy *My Family, My Friends, My Food: Recipes Celebrating People and Life* for authentic yet updated tastes of Texas, Mexico, and the world.

Susan Spicer

Welcome to My Table

It is set and the menu includes a lifetime of recipes. I am so happy that you,
my family and friends, are here to enjoy this feast with me.
Dive in and let's celebrate life!

In 1981 when I was in seventh grade and took my first cooking class,
I never imagined that eleven years later I would be enrolled in a college
where the only classes I attended were cooking. I never even dreamed that
in fourteen years I would be teaching my own class and in fifteen years
running a cooking school! That first class at Mount Sacred Heart School
was by no means my first encounter with the technical aspects of cooking.
At a much younger age, while my classmates were filling out their
Scholastic Book order forms for mysteries, adventures, and joke books, I
was placing orders for all of the children's cookbooks and beginner's
guides to cooking. Many of those books still sit on my shelves.

I remember on weekends and school holidays studying those books and
making things like Baked Pork and Bean Casserole, Fresh Broccoli with
Mild Cheese Sauce, Individual Pizzas, where rolled out biscuits formed the
crust (one of my favorites), and a Spring Bonnet Cake that was decorated
with gumdrops. From these first books, I learned the definitions of many
cooking terms. I also learned that sometimes the recipes were too simple,
or maybe I should say they lacked specifics. For example, a recipe
for some cookies I was attempting called for cloves.
Finding a tin of whole cloves in my mother's spice cabinet, I proceeded
to add a teaspoon. Once the first batch was out of the oven, I dove in to
sample my first homemade cookies. I was disappointed, to say the least,
when I bit into a clove. I told myself that's how they were supposed to taste,
excusing it as a "grown-up's" recipe. Later my mother came home from
work, and I proudly handed her one of the "grown-up" tasting cookies.
The look on her face told me that grown-ups didn't like them either.

I showed my mom the recipe, and she told me that it was the book's fault, of course! (To this day, I'm still not that big on cloves.) This failed baking experience did not turn me off to the world of pâtisserie, however. I remember spending many evenings in the kitchen with my mother baking sweet little morsels. My mother enjoys baking and is quite good at it. She likes it for the same reason that I now dislike it: baking is an exact science. But I'm getting ahead of myself.

My preliminary gastronomic experiences were highly influenced by my two grandmothers. Alicia (a.k.a. Uelita) seemed to live her life in the kitchen, catering to every single member of her family. The pots and pans on her stove were always filled with delicacies, from chiles rellenos to cabrito. Her table always had room for an extra person; actually, there were two tables in her kitchen, which meant room for many extras. Uelita was a wealth of information (not only about food but also about what was going on in town). My fondest memory is of the time she taught me how to make tamales, a week before she died.

Granny, my mother's mother, was a good cook, but she didn't really spend time in the kitchen until after my grandfather died. He was the chef, literally. My understanding is that Elma didn't do that much cooking until after his untimely death. From that point on, she was the master of the kitchen, putting into practice all that she had learned from her Mexican childhood in conjunction with the Texas cooking she had seen my grandfather prepare. Now that I think about it, my foundation in cross-cultural cuisine probably comes from her. Granny liked baking, and her specialty was pies. She made the best crust I have ever tasted. Unfortunately, I never got her secret. Granny's love of baking must have rubbed off on my mother.

My mother is very methodical and says that as long as she has a good recipe to follow, she can make anything. When it comes to baking, she always has a recipe and the results are fabulous. When I was in primary school, she was always a room mother. While the other mothers provided store-bought sweets for class parties, Mom's were always homemade. They may not have been the most beautiful of the desserts present, but when it came to taste, they were by far the best. One bite and you could tell they were made with love. As I look back, I realize that my basic philosophy on food and flavor comes from my mother. It doesn't have to be the prettiest, but if it's made with love, it will be the best. Thanks, Mom!

My early baking experiences weren't confined to my mother's kitchen. I had one other great influence, Aunt Mague. My father's older sister, Mague Flores-Nutt learned how to cook from her mother, my Uelita. Though raised in the Mexican kitchen, my Aunt Mague's cooking went beyond that cuisine. Her spaghetti and her cakes are what I remember most. Aunt Mague made beautiful cakes, and the first time I saw one, I immediately knew I had to learn how to make them myself.

After my mother chauffeured me all over town to every cake store in the city, I had the best equipped cake decorating set around— Wilton's® stocks were up that year! It included every imaginable tip, all sizes of pastry bags and spatulas, and so many food colors it put a rainbow to shame. My "classes" then started with Aunt Mague. On the weekends, she showed me how to fill and hold a pastry bag. I learned the function and use of each tip. She even taught me how to combine colors to achieve the shade I wanted. And for a while I was a cake decorating fool, making one for every occasion possible. I must admit, I wasn't that bad. I even made cakes for showers and weddings. Once I made a cake with the Eiffel Tower on it for a friend who was being transferred to Paris. This is where the story of my very first business begins.

From grades 1 to 8, I was instructed by the Sisters of the Sacred Heart of Jesus of St. Jacut. Some of the sisters are still a special part of my life to this day. I asked one of them to be my confirmation sponsor when I was a freshman in high school. This same nun, a year later, was transferred to Paris, France, and I made the Eiffel Tower cake for her. I presented it to Sr. Ernestine at a surprise going-away party that I hosted. Sylvia Herrera, one of my former teachers, was a guest at the party. After devouring the cake, she suggested that I go into the pâtisserie business. In hindsight I'm sure that she meant sometime in the future, probably after college. I, however, did not take it that way. By the end of the next day, I had designed my business cards and was being chauffeured, once again by my mother, to the office supply store to have them printed. Within seven working days my first business was opened: Michael's Cakes etc. I still have a box of the cards in a drawer in my room.

There I was, a freshman in high school running my own baking business. To start, I raided my mother's recipe file and copied down, on index cards, the confectioneries I liked the most in order to start my own files. To this day my mother still says that her recipe collection has never been the same since "THE pillaging!" The phrase "I used to know where it was until you . . ." is burned into my mind forever. That old metal filing box still sits on my desk at home. It is filled not only with recipes but also with the cost of ingredients (at the time), and specifics about the likes and dislikes of my customers. Not bad for a thirteen-year-old. Recently I came across a bill (made out to my mother) that had written on the bottom, in my adolescent handwriting, the phrase "franchizes available."
Even then I knew I had places to go.

The first, and the majority, of the customers of Michael's Cakes etc. were family. Here it's important to tell you that almost all of my family lives in Laredo, Texas, whereas I live in San Antonio.

At the time, the speed limit was 55 mph, and Laredo was about three hours away. Almost every weekend I would load up my mother's car with cakes, cookies, candies, and more, and she would drive me to Laredo to make my deliveries! Besides cookies and candies being part of the "etc.," homemade Mexican chorizo eventually found its way to my menu.

Soon I had requests that required full catering services to go along with the cakes. Some even included official functions for the city of San Antonio. I tried to accommodate as many orders as I could while still going to high school and working out of my mother's kitchen. Eventually, however, Michael's Cakes etc. grew too big for me to handle, and I had to close it down. According to my parents, my education was more important.

Throughout the rest of high school, I continued to dabble here and there in the culinary arts but did not really share my talents with the public again until I was in college. I never actually cared for college, or for that matter, school in general. I liked the learning part. It was the homework and tests that never really fascinated me! While at university, I floundered here and there in a sea of majors. Had they offered a degree in a field entitled "Potpourri," I would have graduated years earlier. It was during one of these college semesters that I had to call upon my culinary talents once again.

After briefly enduring what I considered to be an uninteresting course load, I decided to drop all of my fall classes, unbeknownst to my parents, who happened to be footing the bill for my college tuition. At the same time, I was planning a trip to New York with my cousin Marci to visit family and celebrate the New Year. To make a long story short, when my parents found out what I had done, I was given the choice of paying them back for the semester (including books) or not going to New York. I quickly started making tamales and White Chocolate Walnut Fudge (a recipe I had developed a year or so earlier and which is now famous)

14

and peddling them to everyone I knew. I not only paid my parents back but also went to New York with pockets full of cash! This trip to New York changed my life forever.

Although I loved cooking from an early age, I never really thought of making a career out of it. It had always been just a pleasant and amusing hobby. Up to this point I never really had much culinary experience in the real world. We live in a society that associates certain genders with certain jobs, and what I knew of cooking came from watching my mother, grandmothers, and housekeepers, in the home kitchen. Even at school the cafeteria was run by the nuns, headed up by Sr. Philomena Rios. Consequently, I thought cooking was a world populated only by women. This concept changed completely during my New York trip.

Until 1991, I had never heard of The Culinary Institute of America (CIA) in Hyde Park, New York. Nor did I know that it was considered the best culinary school in the world. It wasn't until a friend of mine, Celina Rios Mullan, heard how much I disliked "normal" college and learned of my passion for food that she told me about the school. Talk about timing! Before leaving on my trip, I called the CIA and inquired about tours. I was informed that they were going to be closed for the Christmas holidays and would reopen the day after Marci and I were scheduled to return home. I went ahead and scheduled a tour and then immediately called Marci and told her that our itinerary had changed; we would be staying in New York for a few more days than originally planned. The day that the CIA reopened, my cousin Dennis "Brick" Pennock drove me there. It was love at first sight. By May of that year (1992) I was enrolled and attending classes. What followed were two of the best years of my life.

The curriculum at the Culinary Institute of America is based on a progressive learning year (a.k.a. PLY) with an externship at a "real" restaurant smack-dab in the middle. When it was time for my externship,

I took a look at various places. Some of my options included a private club in Hong Kong and the White House. During this decision time, I recalled that Regina Keever, the wife of one of my father's friends, had opened a restaurant in New Orleans, Louisiana, called Bayona. Her partner was a chef, Susan Spicer, an up-and-coming culinary luminary. A bit of research helped me decide that Bayona was where I wanted to go. After several conversations with Regina, I finally got to talk with Susan. And after hounding Susan (a practice of mine that she has become more than familiar with), she finally agreed to hire me. Before I actually started working, I visited the restaurant in order to familiarize myself with it. Longtime friend Lance Leaming went with me to meet Chef Spicer. If you are familiar with New Orleans, you will understand when I tell you that I don't remember anything about that weekend!

I arrived at Bayona knowing nothing about the industrial kitchen and how it operated. Fortunately for me, Chef Spicer was not there my first week so I had a little time to acclimate myself. I thoroughly enjoyed working in the cramped kitchen of Bayona and consider my time spent there one of the highlights of my career. I rotated through all the stations of the kitchen, whether ready or not. On one occasion, I was scheduled to work the vegetable station on the hot line. The person at this station was responsible for making sure that hot plates were ready and counted out for the tables that were soon to be served. The job also entailed putting the proper vegetables and starches on each plate. I don't think I was quite ready for this appointment, because at one peak moment during service Susan said, "Move!" and took my spot on the line! Fortunately, it was the first and only time.

Susan Spicer, being not only a great chef but also a wonderful woman, allowed me to experience all aspects of the restaurant business. During my time at Bayona, I was not only assigned to every position in the kitchen but also worked in the bakery and in the front of the house as well. Susan was the second woman in my life (my mother being the first) who had a major influence in my culinary journey. I am proud to say that she is now not only a mentor but also a friend. I think that Susan would agree that I have come a long way from that arrogant CIA student who first set foot in her kitchen.

It was a sad day for me when I had to leave Bayona and return to the CIA to resume my education. Chef Spicer said that I could stay if I wanted, but I knew that I had to go back and finish what I had started. I graduated from The Culinary Institute of America on January 28, 1994, with several honors bestowed upon me. Then came the real world!

After graduation, I returned home to San Antonio and eventually became the Executive Chef of Barcelona's Mediterranean Cafe. There my skills sharpened, and I truly put into practice the concept of "cross-cultural cuisine," creating favorites like Mediterranean Nachos and Moroccan Guacamole. It was at this point that my career shifted into high speed. On a daily basis I was asked to teach cooking classes, make television and radio appearances, give newspaper and magazine interviews, and donate my time and talents to various nonprofit fund-raisers. Looking back, it was too much too soon. I was becoming a star before my light was ready to shine.

During my time at Barcelona's, I co-founded an event called "Nutcracker Sweets." It is now an annual celebration that honors chefs and the holiday desserts they create. The proceeds from this gala benefit the Battered Women's Shelter in San Antonio, Texas. Creating this event brought me back to my pâtisserie roots and allowed me to meet great chefs from all over the country, creating a fantastic network. It has also provided me a way to give back to the community in which I was raised.

After leaving Barcelona's, I was asked to help open a cooking school and gourmet store in downtown San Antonio. Next, I consulted with a restaurant in upstate New York. I returned to San Antonio for the position of Executive Chef and Food and Beverage Manager at a "Small Luxury Hotel" on the banks of the San Antonio River. During this time, I continued to teach classes and make special guest appearances. I was even guest chef aboard the *American Orient Express* for two weeks, and in October of 1998 I had the honor of cooking at the renowned James Beard House in New York City.

Before that, however, on October 17, 1997, I started my own food manufacturing business. I began creating, producing, and selling my own line of gourmet food products. I started with three dessert sauces, and more than five years later have over thirty products that I market and sell internationally. They include spice blends, roasted garlic, cooking sauces, jellies, salad dressings, pickles, dip mixes, chipotle mayonnaise and mustard, and an incredible Bloody Mary mix. Since late 1999, that's where my focus has been. My days are spent in the test kitchen and manufacturing plant. I choose jars and design labels. I go from the Fancy Food shows to the National Gourmet Markets. I travel to fairs all over the country and offer samples of my foods in tiny gourmet stores. I have learned that owning a business means that you are everything from the shipper to the receptionist, the delivery man to the bookkeeper, the boss to the employee.

The name of my food manufacturing company is Mis En Place, French for "everything in its place." In culinary circles it refers to having everything you need for a particular dish gathered and ready to go (from ingredients to pots and pans). The products are marketed under the name "Chef Michael H. Flores." In the first year or so of business, my drive was towards wholesale accounts. Currently, the company's main focus is retail.

Mis En Place has turned into a "dot com" company. My time now is spent traveling and promoting my products directly to the consumer. I can't go on without giving credit to a colleague of mine, Lynn Nicklo. Before I started Mis En Place, she started Hösgoods, a gourmet company dedicated to garlic. Much of the knowledge of this business comes from her. In the first years of Mis En Place, Lynn held my hand and taught me all that she knew. If you are interested in taking a look at my gourmet products, you can do so via the World Wide Web at *www.chefmichael.com*.

I have guided you through my culinary background so that you will understand and appreciate the roots from which both this book and I have grown. This cookbook is a compilation of recipes created through the years for my immediate family, and for you, my family of customers. It includes dishes that friends have made and that I have enjoyed. I've added versions of recipes that I remember Granny, Uelita, and Mom serving at their tables to family and friends.

Writing this book has been a labor of love. And you will understand when I say it has been a lifetime in the making. Food excites me! It's something that all people have in common and that unites us as a global community. It sustains our existence while nourishing the body and enriching the soul. This book exemplifies my philosophy that good food begins with pure love. Cook these recipes while celebrating life and the people in it! ¡Buen Provecho!

Michael H. Flores

(Author's Note: All through school I would write papers that contained sentences starting with the word "and." My teachers always corrected me saying that this was grammatically incorrect. I would recite a list of books where the authors had begun many sentences with the word "and." I was told that that was the author's privilege and when I wrote a book I could do the same thing. Well, guess what, teachers! I have, and I did!)

Getting Started

Here is a basic list of things that will help when preparing the recipes in this book. They are notes that will allow the final outcome of your dish to taste more like the ones I created in my kitchen. If you give attention to what I say here, the outcome will be as if you, your family, and friends are eating in my home, at my table.

- Read the "chapter starter" before attempting a recipe. It may give you some insight into where I was coming from when I created the dish.

- I use ONLY kosher salt. I find it to be mellower than regular, iodized salt; remember to use kosher salt when making recipes where salt is one of the ingredients.

- When pepper is called for, use freshly ground black pepper. I have an electric coffee grinder that I use only for spices, which is what I use to grind my whole peppercorns. Do a few tablespoons of peppercorns at a time as needed. The difference really is quite noticeable. You can control the size of the grind (fine to coarse) by the amount of time you hold down the button.

- You will notice that in many dishes I use the juice of a lemon or lime. That's a great way to cut through any fats in the recipe that may be coating your tongue and thus allow all the flavors of the food to shine through. This is an important hint to remember and to apply in your daily cooking.

- Oftentimes, canned tomatoes are a better choice than fresh ones—unless you happen to grown your own and are making a recipe that calls for tomatoes in the peak season! When I use canned tomatoes, I prefer Cento® brand chef's cut. It is a great-tasting tomato in a thicker than normal juice, and the tomatoes are cut more into strips than diced.

- Maggi Seasoning® is a liquid flavor enhancer that comes in a dark brown bottle with a bright yellow label with red lettering.

Lately, I've seen it at more and more grocery stores. If you can't find it there, try your local Asian or Latin market. (Note: It comes in a variety of flavors, and any one will do for the recipes where it is called for.)

- In almost every recipe you will notice that I say "taste and adjust seasonings." This is because we all have different taste buds and different preferences for how we like our food seasoned. You may like more salt than I do, or vice versa. In any case, season—or don't season— to your liking.

- The term **CHIFFONADE** refers to leafy vegetables or herbs that are cut into fine shreds. This is accomplished by gathering the item tightly and finely slicing it with a large chef's knife.

- I use various layman's terms to describe how things should be cut. Here is what I mean by each. Please note that unless otherwise noted these are approximations and by no means need to be perfect.

  finely minced—usually used in reference to garlic, this should be a tiny cut, like running through a garlic press

  mince—cut very small

  dice—pieces cut to about 1/4-inch square

  chop—about 1/2-inch pieces or so

  rough chop—just chop it up into pieces, maybe 3/4-inch or so

- If you don't already have one, go to the grocery store and buy a little scale. It really does not need to be able to weigh more than a pound. I say this because oftentimes I give units of measure in net weight, and unless we are talking about water, "a pint is not a pound the world around!"

- After reading the above, know that when I give something in ounces, it means net weight. When I list ounces in references to a canned item, it is how the product typically is sold, and how the measurement is listed on the label of the can.

- When heating oil for sautéing you can tell that it is ready when you look across the surface of it and see it "rippling." Kind of the same way a Texas highway looks at one o'clock in the afternoon in July!

- To test if oil is ready for frying, stick a chopstick or wooden skewer in it. You should see a lot of tiny bubbles around the stick, as if it were frying.

- One of the hardest things to master is knowing when a piece of meat is cooked to your desired doneness (especially if it is not rare or well done). Here is a little secret that I do when cooking individual portions. Choose the piece that you plan to serve to yourself and cut deep into the back of it, open it, and check to see the doneness. If serving beef medallions, you can even cut the whole thing in half to check the temperature and serve it up as two smaller medallions.

- When cooking larger pieces of meat (e.g., a roast), you are going to need a thermometer if you are not quite sure.

- When cooking pork, remember that trichinosis is virtually nonexistent. It is no longer necessary to cook the heck out of it to make it safe! It is perfectly okay, and much more pleasing to the palate, to serve it pink to rosy gray.

- If there are certain pieces or cuts of meat that you are looking for (e.g., semi-boneless quail or boneless duck breasts, just to name a couple) but cannot find at your local grocery store, specialty store, or even butcher, try the local meat purveyor in your city. These are the companies that sell to restaurants. You can find them in the phone book. Oftentimes, they also sell directly to the public. As a last resort, ask the chef at your favorite restaurant if he or she can get it for you.

- When using nutmeg, use only whole nutmeg, grated on a nutmeg grater. The whole nutmeg lasts indefinitely and the flavor cannot be duplicated by using ground nutmeg in the tin. If you don't have a nutmeg grater, go buy one now!

- When I use the term "sheet pan," I am referring to what is commonly known as a cookie tray, with four very shallow sides.

- Here, I need everyone to sit down! There are a few recipes in this book that call for lard. That's right . . . LARD! Everything has its place in the kitchen, and lard definitely has one. As long as that is not a problem for you, great. If it is, either get over it or don't make the recipe!!! For those recipes that call for lard, there is no substitution. Remember, I am passing these notes on to you so that they will taste at your table the way they taste at mine. You don't have to eat it every day, and basically, in all recipes, the lard stays in the pan and is only helping to season the dish.

- In some recipes, I call for seeded, fresh tomatoes. Here is how: Cut the tomato into quarters (top to bottom). Cut the centers out, including the seeds. Discard the centers or save them for a stock. This procedure does not have to be perfect. If there are a few seeds remaining, don't sweat it.

- Oftentimes, when I talk about vegetables and herbs, I use a unit of measurement called bunches. "Bunches" refers to how they are gathered, presented, and purchased at your local grocery store. For example, when I say "a bunch of beets," I mean go to the produce section of your store and grab up a bundle or bunch of beets. When I refer to a bunch of herbs, the same thing goes. In many recipes where herbs are used, I say "2/3 ounce, net weight." That is because that's how they are found at my local store.

- I only use Parmigiano-Reggiano Parmesan cheese.

- Finally, the book that you have in your hand is NOT a Bible. It was not given to me at the top of a mountain, carved in stone. It is only a guide. Feel free to change the recipes to your liking. For example, if you prefer parsley to cilantro, switch it; lemons instead of limes, make the change. Use a sauce on vegetables instead of fish, or try pork instead of beef. Granted, basic techniques need to be followed, but be creative and add your own special flair. Cooking should be fun, not a hassle.

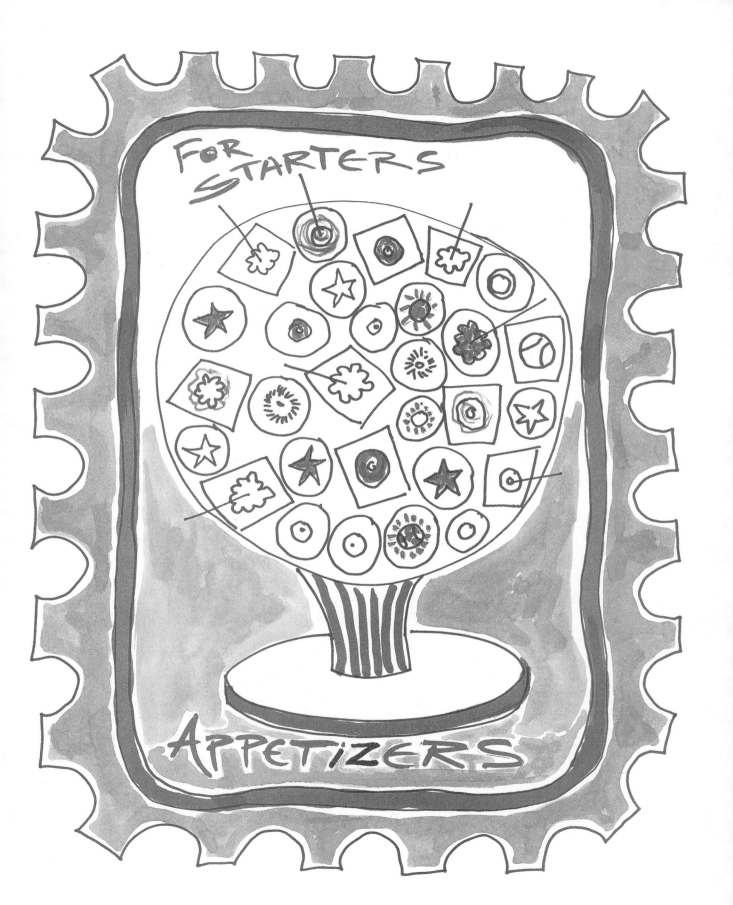

*H*ors d'oeuvre and appetizers are my favorite part of any meal, except, of course, the joy of sharing food with my friends—I absolutely love to graze on food. The hors d'oeuvre (which means "outside of the meal" and should never be written with an "s" as there is only one meal, or oeuvre) is enjoyed as everyone arrives at the party. The excitement is high, guests are saying their hellos, mingling, catching up, and conversing with everyone as they enjoy all the delicious pre-dinner snacks the host and hostess have prepared.

Here is the perfect chance to play with food and experiment, having fun with flavors and ingredients. There are no real rules, and anything goes as long as it is bite-sized or at least two-bite-sized! You can do any number of combinations. When planning my hors d'oeuvre, I try to keep them in odd numbers, starting with a minimum of three and working from there. Note that they do not have to be complicated. They can be as simple as marinated vegetables.

When presenting these pre-dinner munchies, I choose decorative platters and bowls for serving. I don't pay too much attention to over-the-top, gorgeous presentations. Don't get me wrong: I want it to look good! However, once that first piece is taken or that delicious spread is dipped into, you no longer have that fabulous-looking dish that took hours of painstaking work. In the end, it's the taste that everyone will remember.

Appetizers, however, are meant to be eaten at the table, before the entrée is served. When throwing a dinner party, I tend to serve too much food or too many courses! One way I solve that problem (although some people don't consider it a problem) is to make my appetizer count as either the vegetable or the starch. By serving some sort of pasta, potato, rice, or vegetable as the appetizer, I don't have to include it with the main course.

I consider appetizers "fun food." When eating at a restaurant, I like to order a bunch of appetizers and no entrée. This way I get to nosh on a number of items and enjoy some different, often unusual dishes that the chef has created. Another fun thing to do when it comes to appetizers is to have everyone at the table order something different, take a bite, and pass it to the right. This only works, though, if you are dining with good friends!

So when it comes to dealing with food, FOR STARTERS, have fun. It's your chance to experiment and try those recipes that have always sounded delicious. Even if the recipe is intended to be an entrée, cut the portions into smaller sizes, and voilà, you have a starter.

For Starters

Spanakopita	27
New Potatoes with Escargot, Cilantro Pesto & Brie	28
Mediterranean Nachos	29
Spinach & Oyster Empanadas with Fennel Aïoli	30
Savory Chipotle Three Cheese Cake	31
Cold Spring Rolls	32
Eggplant & Parmesan Purée	33
Steak Tartare	33
Mediterranean Torta	34
Artichokes, Mushrooms & Peppers with Cumin	35
Cilantro Shrimp	36
Crayfish Sundried Tomato Pâté	36
Scallop Seviche	37
Roquefort Custards	37
Gâteaux d'Aubergines on a Lentil Salad with Feta Cheese & Sundried Tomato Aïoli	38
Champagne Cured Salmon	40
Cumin Carrot & Potato Spread with Toasted Pita Points	41
Mini Ravioli with Sundried Tomato Pesto Atop Grilled Portobello Mushrooms	42
Leeks & Feta in Filo	43
Shrimp with Garlic & Vegetables	44
Roasted Garlic Flan with Spiced Pecans	45

Spanakopita

(Spinach and Cheese Pie)

*This Greek delicacy is one of my favorites and can be served a
number of ways besides sandwiched in filo as described here. Try baking it
in a greased pan without the filo layers. After it has cooled, scoop it out into
mini filo shells, found in the freezer section of your grocery store. I must
warn you, if preparing it this way, make extra filling. It is so addictive you
may just eat it all up before your shells are complete!*

Sauté the white and green onions and garlic in the olive oil for 3 minutes. Add the spinach and herbs. Stir until the spinach has wilted and the liquid has evaporated. Cool.

Beat the eggs in a bowl. Add the 2 cheeses and the spinach mixture (making sure to drain any extra liquid). Next add the nutmeg, salt, and pepper. Taste the filling and adjust the seasonings if necessary.

Brush a 13×9-inch pan with some of the melted butter. Lay out a sheet of filo, brush with butter, and sprinkle lightly with 1 tablespoon of bread crumbs. Repeat 5 times and top with a sheet of filo. Place these filo layers in the pan (sides will come up).

Pour the spinach mixture over the filo layers.

Again, lay out a sheet of filo, brush with butter, and sprinkle lightly with 1 tablespoon of bread crumbs. Repeat 5 times and top with a sheet of filo. Place these filo layers over the spinach mixture and tuck the ends in. Brush the top with butter.

Bake for 1 hour at 375 degrees or until the pie is golden brown, crisp and puffed up. Cut into squares or diamonds.

Serve hot immediately or cool to serve at room temperature.

Ingredients

1 white onion, chopped
4 green onions, sliced
5 garlic cloves, roughly chopped
4 tablespoons olive oil
2 pounds spinach, julienned
2 tablespoons minced dill
2 tablespoons minced parsley
4 eggs
10 ounces feta cheese, crumbled
1/4 cup grated Parmesan cheese
Pinch of nutmeg
1 teaspoon kosher salt
2 teaspoons coarsely ground
   black pepper
12 sheets filo
1/2 cup (1 stick) butter, melted
1 cup unflavored bread crumbs

New Potatoes with Escargot, Cilantro Pesto & Brie

This little hors d'oeuvre is quite delicious. Do not be turned off by the escargot. If you have never eaten them, this is a great way to have them for the first time. Try the Cilantro Pesto in other recipes besides this one. It's great tossed with grilled chicken and pasta.

Potatoes
10 to 12 new or red potatoes
2 tablespoons salt

Cilantro Pesto
1 bunch (about 4 ounces)
   cilantro
1/2 cup pumpkin seeds (pepitas)
5 garlic cloves
Juice of 1 lime
1 teaspoon salt
1 teaspoon freshly ground
   black pepper
1/3 cup corn oil
1 cup shredded Manchego
   cheese

Assembly
1 (7-ounce) can cooked escargot,
   [about 18 to 20 count] drained
   and rinsed
Brie cheese, sliced about
  2 inches long
Cilantro, minced, for garnish

Potatoes
Cut the potatoes in half lengthwise. Slice a small bit off of the bottoms so that they will sit well.

Drop into salted boiling water and cook for approximately 25 minutes or just until soft. Cooking time will depend on the size of the potato so please watch.

When soft, drain and let stand until cool to the touch. Scoop out a hole in the center of each slice—do not go all the way down. Set aside until ready to use.

Cilantro Pesto
Cut the stems off the cilantro. Place the cilantro, pumpkin seeds, garlic, lime juice, salt, pepper, corn oil and cheese in a food processor or blender and purée until smooth (add more oil if needed). Taste and adjust seasonings with salt if necessary.

Assembly
Place the potatoes in a shallow baking dish. Place an escargot in each potato and top with a heaping spoonful of pesto followed by a slice of cheese. Bake in a 350-degree oven until the cheese is melted. Serve with the cilantro sprinkled on top.

Mediterranean Nachos

I created these nachos when I was working as the Executive Chef in a Mediterranean restaurant in San Antonio, Texas. Not a day went by that someone did not come in and ask if we had nachos! Finally I decided to do something about it. I took the basic concept of the nacho, used pita bread, and topped it with ingredients common to all regions of the Mediterranean. My customers fell in love with them. I even served them at an event when the International Association of Culinary Professionals met in San Antonio in 1995. Julia Child herself stopped and tried them. She raved about the nachos the rest of the evening. For this recipe, I ask that you bear with the chef in me—there are no amounts listed for the ingredients! It all depends on how many people you are serving and how much you like each ingredient. Don't worry; trust yourself! You really can't mess these up.

SERVES A VARIABLE NUMBER

Nachos
Pita bread
Olive oil
Cumin
Garlic powder
Eggplant & Parmesan Purée (page 33)
Feta cheese, as desired
Kalamata olives, pitted and sliced
Sundried tomatoes in olive oil, julienned
Harissa Sauce
Gyro meat (or browned ground lamb)
Mozzarella cheese, shredded

Harissa Sauce
5 red peppers, roasted
1 teaspoon ground cardamom
1 teaspoon ground coriander
1 tablespoon ground cumin
1 teaspoon cayenne pepper
1 tablespoon lemon juice
1/4 bunch cilantro
3 garlic cloves
Salt and black pepper to taste

Cut a pita bread into 6 wedges. Place on a baking sheet and drizzle with olive oil; sprinkle with cumin and garlic powder. Toast in a 350-degree oven until crisp, approximately 15 to 20 minutes. Cool.

Spread each "chip" with Eggplant & Parmesan Purée. Next, place a desired amount of feta cheese, kalamata olives, sundried tomatoes and harissa sauce on top of the "chips." Julienne the gyro meat and add to the nachos. Top with mozzarella cheese.

Bake until the cheese has melted and begun to brown.

Harissa Sauce
Place the peppers, spices, lemon juice, cilantro, garlic and salt and pepper in a food processor and purée until smooth. Adjust seasonings. Refrigerate until serving time.

Chef's Note
I know that you will have problems finding the gyro meat. I suggest you go to your favorite Mediterranean restaurant that serves gyros and buy the meat directly from them. I know that all of this sounds complicated, but, trust me, the end result is well worth it.

Spinach & Oyster Empanadas with Fennel Aïoli

Don't be intimidated by this recipe—especially if you like oysters and fennel. The hardest part is gathering the ingredients. Once you master the concept of making empanadas in this particular fashion, the possibilities are endless.

MAKES EIGHT LARGE OR EIGHTEEN SMALL EMPANADAS

Spinach Filling
4 tablespoons butter
2 tablespoons chopped shallots
6 garlic cloves, minced
12 ounces baby spinach leaves, washed and dried
3 tablespoons flour
1 cup milk
Dash of nutmeg
1 teaspoon salt
1 teaspoon black pepper

Oysters
18 raw oysters (about 1 pound)
2 tablespoons flour
1 teaspoon salt
1/4 teaspoon cayenne pepper

Fennel Aïoli
1 egg
1 egg yolk
1 tablespoon water
5 garlic cloves
Juice of 1 lemon
2 tablespoons white vinegar
1 teaspoon prepared mustard
1 teaspoon salt
1 teaspoon hot red pepper sauce (like Tabasco)
1 tablespoon anisette
2 cups peanut oil
1 1/2 heaping cups (about) coarsely chopped fresh fennel

Assembly
2 sheets puff pastry

Spinach Filling
Melt the butter in a large sauce pot. Add the shallots and garlic and sauté for about 1 minute. Add the spinach and continue cooking until the spinach is wilted and the moisture has evaporated, approximately 4 minutes.

Stir in the flour and cook for 3 minutes, stirring continuously and scraping the bottom of the pot. Stir in the milk, nutmeg, salt and pepper and cook over low heat for 10 minutes, stirring occasionally. Remove from the heat and set aside.

Oysters
Drain the oysters and dry on paper towels. Toss with the flour, salt and cayenne pepper. Refrigerate until needed.

Fennel Aïoli
Place the egg, egg yolk, water, garlic, lemon juice, vinegar, mustard, salt, pepper sauce and anisette in a food processor and purée for about 1 minute or until light and fluffy. Add the peanut oil very slowly, processing until an emulsion forms. Add the chopped fennel and pulse until chopped and well-combined. Taste and adjust seasonings if necessary. Refrigerate until needed.

Assembly
Defrost the puff pastry according to the package directions. To make 8 appetizer-size empanadas, cut each sheet into 4 equal squares. For 18 hors d'oeuvre-size empanadas, cut each sheet into 9 equal squares and roll them out to pieces no smaller than 5-inch squares.

Place an oyster in the center of each square (2 if making larger ones) and top with a tablespoon of the spinach mixture (2 tablespoons if making larger ones). Brush a bit of water on the edges and fold over, forming a triangle. Using the tines of a fork, press the edges to seal the empanada.

Put the finished empanadas on a baking tray lined with parchment paper and bake in a 400-degree oven for 20 minutes or until golden brown. Serve with the aïoli.

Savory Chipotle Three Cheese Cake

This recipe was made for a cooking demonstration I was asked to do at a Home and Garden Show. The method is that of a basic cheese cake, with a twist. It's delicious not only by itself as an appetizer, but also served with smoked salmon or a big tossed salad for brunch.

Crust

Crush the chips finely. Mix the chips with butter and spices. Press the mixture into the prepared pan. Wrap the outside of a 9-inch springform pan with foil, shaping an extended collar; do not allow the foil to extend inside the pan.

Three-Cheese Filling

Sauté the garlic and onions in the corn oil for 4 minutes over medium-low heat. Remove from the heat and stir in the cilantro. Set aside.

Beat the egg yolks until thick and lemon-colored. Break up the cheeses and beat into the yolks until smooth. Add the lime juice, chipotle chiles, salt, cornstarch and sautéed mixture.

In a separate bowl, beat the egg whites until stiff but not dry. Gently fold into the cheese mixture. Pour the filling over the crust and top with the pecan mixture.

Place in a baking pan and place in hot water that comes 1/2 to 3/4 of the way up the sides of the springform pan.

Bake in a 350-degree oven for 1 hour, or until set. Turn the oven off and leave in the closed oven for 1 hour longer. Remove from the oven and cool before serving.

This cake can be prepared a day or two before serving. Store in the refrigerator. Keep in the pan until ready to serve.

Pecan Topping

Melt the butter in an ovenproof sauté pan over medium heat. Stir in the honey. Add the Worcestershire sauce, pepper sauce, salt and pecans and stir until the pecans are well-coated.

Place in a 350-degree oven for 10 minutes—checking after 5 minutes. Remove from the oven and allow to cool for 10 to 15 minutes. Spoon out with a slotted spoon, leaving any extra liquid in the pan.

Crust

2 big handfuls tortilla chips
2 tablespoons butter, melted
1/2 teaspoon cumin
1/2 teaspoon chile powder

Three-Cheese Filling

5 garlic cloves, minced
4 green onions, sliced
1 tablespoon corn oil
1/4 cup chopped cilantro
5 eggs, separated
16 ounces cream cheese, softened
8 ounces goat cheese, softened
8 ounces queso fresco or feta cheese, softened
Juice of 2 limes
3 to 5 chipotle chiles in adobo sauce, minced
1 teaspoon salt
2 tablespoons cornstarch

Pecan Topping

1 tablespoon butter
2 tablespoons honey
1 teaspoon Worcestershire sauce
1 teaspoon hot red pepper sauce (like Tabasco)
Pinch of salt
1 cup chopped pecans

Cold Spring Rolls

MAKES A VARIABLE NUMBER

Spring Rolls

Rice paper (found in some
grocery stores or in your local
Asian market)
Red leaf lettuce
Fresh mint leaves
Fresh cilantro
Fresh basil leaves
Thin rice noodles, cooked
Deveined shrimp, cooked and
butterflied
Assortment of vegetables,
julienned: carrots, radishes,
red peppers, cucumbers, green
onions, jicama, etc.

Spicy Peanut Dipping Sauce

1 1/2 cups crunchy peanut butter
1 tablespoon minced ginger
2 garlic cloves, minced
1 (13 1/2-ounce) can coconut milk
or cream
1/2 cup hoisin sauce
Sambal oelek to taste
1/4 cup soy sauce
1/2 cup rice wine vinegar
Juice of 2 oranges
Juice of 1 lime
1/4 cup sesame oil
1 tsp Maggi seasoning

My first experience with spring rolls was while working the pantry station at Bayona. One of the ladies who worked the same station came from Vietnam, where spring rolls come from. She made these as a special one night. I was hooked at first bite. Cold spring rolls, also referred to as summer rolls, are only as good as the ingredients used. Your vegetables and herbs must be fresh. This recipe is a guide on how to make them. Feel free to fill your own rolls with the ingredients of your choice. The one thing I will tell you is to not leave out the cilantro, mint, and basil. They are key ingredients to the overall flavor. Please note that this recipe is one of only two in this book in which I chose to not give ingredient amounts. It all depends on how many you are making! If you are unsure, I suggest that you go overboard with the amounts; you can always toss the leftovers together later in order to create a great salad.

Spring Rolls

Dip the rice papers (1 at a time) into hot water quickly to soften. Lay each rice paper on a clean, flat surface.

Place a piece of the lettuce in the center. Top with a few leaves of the herbs and follow with the rice noodles, shrimp and a couple of pieces of each vegetable (all ingredients should be arranged as for a clock from 9 o'clock to 3 o'clock).

Roll tightly, folding in the sides like a burrito. Place in a container and cover with a damp cloth. Repeat until you have the desired amount. Refrigerate until ready to serve (not more than several hours).

Spicy Peanut Dipping Sauce

Combine the peanut butter, ginger, garlic, coconut milk, hoisin sauce, sambal oelek, soy sauce, vinegar, orange and lime juices, sesame oil and Maggi seasoning in a sauce pot. Simmer over medium-low heat, stirring occasionally. Serve warm or at room temperature.

Eggplant & Parmesan Purée

*This is a simple recipe full of flavor that can be served in a
multitude of ways. Try it as a dip alongside pita points, with tomatoes
as a pasta sauce, even stuffed in chicken or a beef tenderloin
before roasting, or as a filling for ravioli.*

SERVES EIGHT TO TEN

Eggplant Purée

Brush the eggplant with olive oil
and roast in a 375-degree oven
until soft, about 15 to 20 minutes.
Cool. Discard the ends. Place the
eggplant, garlic, parsley, onion,
lemon juice, cheese, salt, pepper
and 1/2 cup olive oil in a food
processor and purée until
smooth. Adjust the seasonings
to taste and refrigerate.

Roasted Garlic

For the roasted garlic, cut the
tops off the garlic. Place on foil
and top with the olive oil. Seal
and roast in a 375-degree oven
for 1 1/4 hours. When cool enough
to handle, squeeze the garlic out
of the skin.

Eggplant Purée

1 eggplant, peeled
Olive oil
3 garlic cloves
1/4 bunch parsley
1/4 red onion
2 tablespoons lemon juice
1 cup grated Parmesan cheese
Salt and freshly ground black
    pepper to taste
1/2 cup olive oil

Roasted Garlic

2 heads garlic
3 tablespoons olive oil

Steak Tartare

*I like steak tartare. In a dish like this you aren't really eating raw
meat. All of those wonderful ingredients that are combined with the meat
take it from raw to denatured. The word "denatured" is the appropriate term
to use here instead of "cooked." Cooking suggests that heat has been
applied, and it has not. In any case, if you are leery, be brave and give this
recipe a chance. The one thing to remember when preparing steak tartare is
that you must use a very high quality, fresh piece of meat.*

SERVES FOUR TO SIX

Place the beef tenderloin on a
cutting board. Cut into chunks
with a large kitchen knife. Mince
until it almost resembles a
coarsely ground beef (do not use
a meat grinder). Combine with
the capers, peppercorns, olives,
cornichons, red onions, anchovy
fillets, Worcestershire sauce,
mustard, egg yolk and vinegar
and mix well. Cover tightly and
refrigerate for several hours
before serving. Garnish with the
parsley and serve with peppered
crackers or toast points.

Ingredients

1 pound fresh beef tenderloin
1/4 cup capers
1/4 cup green peppercorns in
    brine
1/4 cup chopped green olives
1/4 cup minced cornichons
3 tablespoons diced red onions
6 anchovy fillets, flattened
3 tablespoons Worcestershire
    sauce
2 tablespoons Dijon mustard
1 egg yolk
1 tablespoon red wine vinegar
1 tablespoon minced Italian
    parsley

Mediterranean Torta

The National Dairy Association asked me to develop some recipes for them where butter was a key element—not a problem for me! This torta is one of those I created. Here, the butter acts not only as a flavoring agent but also to help firm up the three cheeses used. It can be made several days ahead of time and makes for a beautiful presentation. Once you've made this recipe, try other variations by substituting other ingredients for some of the layers.

Ingredients

2 cups (4 sticks) butter, softened
16 ounces feta cheese, crumbled
8 ounces cream cheese, softened
8 ounces goat cheese, crumbled
1 cup pine nuts, toasted and
    ground
1/4 cup (1/2 stick) butter, softened
1 cup roasted red peppers
1 cup sundried tomatoes
1 cup fresh basil
1 cup chopped kalamata olives
1/4 cup (1/2 stick) butter, almost
    melted

Rub a small amount of oil on the inside of a terrine mold, loaf pan or container of your choice. Line the mold with plastic wrap.

Whip 2 cups butter in an electric mixer. Add the 3 cheeses and mix well. Combine the pine nuts and 1/4 cup butter and pat on the bottom of the mold. Spread a third of the butter-cheese mixture on top. Place the roasted peppers on top and carefully brush with a portion of the melted butter. Place half of the remaining butter-cheese mixtue over the peppers.

Purée the sundried tomatoes and basil in a food processor. Spread the purée on top, forming another layer. Brush the tomato-basil layer with butter. Spread the remainder of the butter-cheese mixture and top with kalamata olives. Brush this final layer with more butter. Refrigerate for several hours until hardened.

To serve, dip the mold into some hot water for a couple of seconds and unmold onto your serving platter. Serve with bread or crackers.

Artichokes, Mushrooms & Peppers with Cumin

In 1994, right after I graduated from the CIA, I was invited to Washington, D.C., to cater a meal for 200 dignitaries. At the time, tapas were all the rage, so that was the theme I chose. My good friend and chef Spero Kannavos from Long Island met me in D.C. to help with the party. It was an experience. The event was to take place in this lady's house, and I told her to please clear out her refrigerator—I was flying in from San Antonio with ice chests full of food and had to store it all. Her idea of "clearing out the refrigerator" was throwing away an old jar of mayonnaise! When I arrived the refrigerator was packed. I was fortunate on two counts: the ice I had traveled with had not melted, and it had just snowed. As Spero and I prepared food, we stored it in the snow on her deck! Unfortunately, after burying the food, there was a fresh snowfall, and we had no clue where our tapas had disappeared to! After digging for a while, we finally found them all (I think). This is one of those items that we served at the party. It's quite easy to make and could even be served atop some mixed greens for a salad.

Place the artichokes, mushrooms, bell pepper, poblano chile, garlic, onion, cumin, salt, pepper, and corn oil in a pot. Cook over medium-high heat for 5 minutes, stirring frequently. Add the vinegar and turn the heat down. Simmer for another 7 minutes, stirring occasionally. Taste and adjust seasonings if necessary. Allow to cool. Refrigerate overnight before serving.

Ingredients

- 1 (14-ounce) can marinated artichoke hearts, drained and quartered
- 8 ounces button mushrooms, cut into halves
- 1 red bell pepper, julienned
- 1 poblano chile, julienned
- 2 garlic cloves, minced
- 1/2 red onion, chopped
- 1 tablespoon ground cumin
- 2 teaspoons salt
- 1 teaspoon freshly ground black pepper
- 3/4 cup corn oil
- 1/4 cup sherry vinegar

Cilantro Shrimp

SERVES SIX TO TEN

Ingredients

5 green onions
1 bunch cilantro with stems included
1 cup freshly squeezed lime juice
2 tablespoons corn oil
2 tablespoons sugar
2 serrano chiles, stems off
1 teaspoon kosher salt
2 pounds cooked peeled shrimp with tails

The first time I made this shrimp dish was for my cousin Eddie's wedding reception. It was a hit! It's very easy to make and works well with the flavorless, frozen, cooked shrimp that is readily available at any store. The shrimp can be marinated a couple of days in advance with no problem. I've yet to try the marinade on anything else, but it would be good on scallops or as a marinade for beef or chicken fajitas.

Place the green onions, cilantro, lime juice, corn oil, sugar, serrano chiles and salt in a blender and blend. Pour the mixture over the shrimp and marinate in the refrigerator overnight.

Crayfish Sundried Tomato Pâté

SERVES FIFTEEN TO TWENTY

Ingredients

1 pound cooked crayfish tails, peeled
1 cup sundried tomatoes, rehydrated
2 pounds cream cheese, softened
8 ounces goat cheese, crumbled
4 green onions
2 sprigs fresh dill
3 sprigs fresh thyme, leaves removed, stems discarded
1 teaspoon hot red pepper sauce
Juice of 1 lemon
Salt to taste
1/4 cup capers
2 tablespoons diced red onions

This is not a pâté in the true sense of the word, but the idea behind it, along with its rich flavor, is similar to one. If you have problems finding crayfish (often spelled crawfish) tails, try using shrimp or smoked salmon. However you make it, it's sure to be a hit at your next party.

Place 1/2 pound of the crayfish in a food processor along with the sundried tomatoes, cheeses, green onions, herbs, pepper sauce, lemon juice and salt and purée until smooth. Remove the mixture to a bowl and stir in the remaining 1/2 pound of the crayfish tails.

Pour into a round bowl lined with plastic wrap, pat down and refrigerate for several hours to overnight. Unmold on a platter and top with the capers and red onions. Serve with crackers.

Scallop Seviche

Seviche is not something I order when I'm out because I never know what kind of fish is used or how fresh it is. I do like making it at home, and it's quite easy to do. In seviche, like steak tartare, the fish becomes denatured (not cooked) in the lime juice and therefore safe to eat. The key here is using very fresh fish. For those of you that don't care for scallops, feel free to substitute with any other fish or shellfish.

Place the scallops, red onions, bell pepper and cilantro in a glass bowl. Add the lime juice, olive oil, vinegar, allspice and peppercorns. Toss the mixture and marinate in the refrigerator for 12 hours to overnight.

SERVES FOUR

Ingredients
1 pound scallops, cut into halves
1/2 red onion, finely diced
1/2 red bell pepper, finely diced
1 small handful chopped cilantro
1 cup fresh lime juice
2 tablespoons olive oil
1 tablespoon apple cider vinegar
1/2 teaspoon allspice
2 tablespoons green peppercorns in brine

Roquefort Custards

This simple custard is great as an appetizer or dessert. Serve it garnished with fresh berries, figs, crisp sliced apples, or juicy pears. Just make sure that whatever accompanies it is fresh and in season. For slightly different flavors try using blue cheese or Gorgonzola.

Place the half-and-half in a microwave and heat just until it starts to boil. Place the eggs, egg yolks, 3 ounces cheese and honey in a blender. Pour in the scalded half-and-half and pulse just until combined. Butter six 4-ounce ramekins, place 1 tablespoon of the crumbled cheese in each one and place the ramekins in a baking pan. Fill the ramekins with the half-and-half mixture and pour hot water in the pan to reach halfway up the sides of the ramekins. Cover and bake at 350 degrees for about 30 minutes or until set. Cool before unmolding. Serve with sliced apples, pears, figs or berries.

SERVES SIX

Ingredients
1 1/2 cups half-and-half
2 eggs
2 egg yolks
3 ounces Roquefort cheese, crumbled
2 tablespoons honey
6 tablespoons crumbled Roquefort cheese

Gâteaux d'Aubergines on a Lentil Salad

This is another one of those involved recipes that requires some time—probably for grocery shopping more than anything. I made this recipe for a demonstration I was asked to do at Whole Foods Market. The finished dish makes a wonderful appetizer or can even be used as a vegetarian entrée. ➤

Eggplant Cakes

1 eggplant
2 tablespoons kosher salt
3 tablespoons olive oil
1 Spanish onion, chopped
1 cup diced mushrooms
3 garlic cloves, minced
2 tablespoons capers, chopped
5 anchovy fillets, chopped
1/4 cup chopped parsley
1/4 cup pine nuts, toasted
Juice of 1/2 lemon
1 tablespoon Dijon mustard
2 cups bread crumbs
1/3 cup Sundried Tomato Aïoli
1 teaspoon coarsely ground
    fresh black pepper
Salt and freshly ground black
    pepper to taste
1/4 cup olive oil
Feta cheese

Gâteau d'Aubergines (Eggplant Cakes)

Peel the eggplant and chop into 1/4-inch pieces. Place in a colander and sprinkle with the kosher salt. Let sit for about an hour. Spread the eggplant on paper towels and pat dry.

Heat 3 tablespoons olive oil in a sauté pan and add the eggplant and onion. Sauté until golden brown and tender, approximately 7 minutes. Add the mushrooms and cook for another 3 minutes, then add the garlic and cook for 1 minute.

Add the capers, anchovies, parsley and pine nuts. Continue to cook another 2 minutes.

Remove from the heat and place in a bowl to cool.

Once the eggplant mixture has cooled down, add the lemon juice, Dijon mustard, bread crumbs, and Aïoli. Mix until well-combined. Add the pepper and taste. Adjust the seasonings with salt and pepper if needed.

Form little cakes that are about 3 inches in diameter and about 1/2 inch thick. Freeze the cakes for an hour.

Heat 1/4 cup olive oil in a sauté pan and carefully add the eggplant cakes (straight out of the freezer). Cook each side for 2 to 3 minutes or until golden brown.

with Feta Cheese & Sundried Tomato Aïoli

If you are concerned that your guests may be leery of eggplant, don't be. The Eggplant Cakes taste almost like meat. If you did not know it was eggplant, you would never guess it. Note that the three components of this recipe are strong enough to stand alone and don't have to be presented as one dish.

Sundried Tomato Aïoli

Place the egg yolks, garlic, lime juice and sundried tomatoes in a food processor and purée until combined and smooth.

With the motor still running, slowly pour in both of the olive oils. Then add the salt and pepper. Taste and adjust the seasonings. Keep refrigerated.

Lentil Salad

Place the lentils in a pot with enough water to cover. Simmer over low heat for 25 minutes, or just until the lentils are tender. They should not be mushy.

Drain the lentils if there is any liquid left and allow to cool.

Put the lentils in a bowl along with the garlic, tomatoes, red onion, olives, and herbs.

In a separate bowl, mix together the mustard, honey, vinegar, salt and pepper. Slowly whisk in the olive oils. Taste and adjust the seasonings.

Pour the vinaigrette and the wine over the lentil mixture and toss together. Taste the salad and adjust the seasonings if necessary. Refrigerate for several hours or overnight.

Assembly

Serve the Eggplant Cakes on top of the Lentil Salad and top each cake with a little of the Sundried Tomato Aïoli and crumbled feta cheese.

Sundried Tomato Aïoli

3 egg yolks
3 garlic cloves
Juice of 1 lime
1/2 cup sundried tomatoes, rehydrated
1 3/4 cups olive oil
1/4 cup extra-virgin olive oil
2 teaspoons kosher salt
2 teaspoons coarsely ground black pepper

Lentil Salad

8 ounces green lentils
2 garlic cloves, minced
2 tomatoes, diced
1/2 red onion, diced
1/2 cup chopped kalamata olives
1/4 cup mixed herbs, chopped
1 tablespoon Dijon mustard
2 tablespoons honey
1/4 cup balsamic vinegar
1 teaspoon kosher salt
2 teaspoons coarsely ground black pepper
3/4 cup olive oil
1/4 cup extra-virgin olive oil
1/4 cup red wine

Champagne Cured Salmon

SERVES FIFTEEN TO TWENTY

If you are a fan of salmon, this is a must. It looks more complicated than it actually is; it just takes time. When I first created this recipe, I used Mumm. No special reason except that it's what the bartender handed me when I walked out of the kitchen and asked him to give me a bottle of Champagne for a recipe I was trying. I don't know if it was luck or if he knew what he was doing, but it was delicious and that's the one I've used ever since. You can use your favorite brand— it's sure to come out just as well.

Ingredients

2 tablespoons allspice berries
2 tablespoons whole cloves
2 tablespoons whole coriander
2 tablespoons black peppercorns
1 bottle Champagne
2 cups packed brown sugar
1 cup kosher salt
1 bunch fresh dill
1 bunch fresh cilantro
1 lime, thinly sliced
1 side of salmon, deboned

Toast the allspice, cloves, coriander and black peppercorns in a sauté pan over medium heat for 3 to 5 minutes—be careful NOT to burn.

Crush the spices with the bottom of a clean sauté pan and combine them with the Champagne, brown sugar, salt, dill and cilantro. Add the lime. Mix well and make sure that the sugar and salt are dissolved.

Pour the mixture over the salmon. Weigh down and refrigerate for 24 hours. Flip the salmon and refrigerate for another 24 hours.

Pour off the liquid and clean the salmon of any large pieces of spices.

Slice the salmon thinly. Wrap tightly in plastic wrap and store in the refrigerator until serving.

Cumin Carrot & Potato Spread with Toasted Pita Points

SERVES EIGHT TO TEN

In the Mediterranean restaurant where I worked for a while we had tapas parties every week in the bar. I had some great times working on those tapas. I would start by walking into the refrigerator to see what we had; this would be followed by research, writing recipes, and, finally, preparing them. This spread is one such creation, made after noticing an abundance of carrots and potatoes. It's easy to make and can be used not only as a dip but also as a base for focaccia or pizza.

Preheat oven to 350 degrees. Cut the potatoes into 1-inch squares. Slice the carrots into 1-inch pieces. Toss the vegetables in the olive oil and 1 teaspoon each cumin, salt, and pepper. Place in a roasting pan and bake for 1 hour.

Place the potatoes and carrots in a food processor along with the garlic, lime juice, olive oil, chipotle chile, cumin, salt and pepper. Purée until smooth.

Serve hot or at room temperature topped with chopped cilantro and pita bread that has been toasted in a 350-degree oven for about 7 minutes and cut into triangles.

Ingredients

1 pound potatoes, peeled
1 pound carrots, peeled
2 tablespoons extra-virgin olive oil
1 teaspoon cumin
1 teaspoon salt
1 teaspoon freshly ground black pepper
1 garlic clove
2 tablespoons fresh lime juice
2/3 cup olive oil
1 chipotle chile in adobo sauce (optional)
2 teaspoons cumin
1 teaspoon salt
1 teaspoon freshly ground black pepper
Chopped cilantro
Pita bread

Mini Ravioli with Sundried Tomato Pesto Atop Grilled Portobello Mushrooms

Serves Four to Six

Ravioli

¹/₂ cup ricotta cheese
¹/₂ cup goat cheese
1 egg
1 tablespoon Italian Seasonings (page 74)
¹/₃ cup plain bread crumbs
Square wonton wraps (approximately 3-inch squares)

Sundried Tomato Pesto

8 ounces sundried tomatoes in oil
5 garlic cloves
1 tablespoon red wine vinegar
¹/₃ cup pine nuts
¹/₂ cup grated Parmesan cheese
¹/₂ cup olive oil
2 teaspoons kosher salt
Juice of 1 lemon
1 teaspoon crushed red pepper flakes

Mushrooms

4 to 6 portobello mushroom caps
1 cup olive oil
¹/₃ cup balsamic vinegar
2 garlic cloves, crushed
2 teaspoons salt
2 teaspoons coarsely ground black pepper

Assembly

Olive oil
Chiffonade of basil

You'll see here how I use Chinese wonton wraps to make Italian ravioli! It really works quite well, and in a matter of minutes you have a great stuffed pasta without all the hassle. Give it a try, not just in this recipe but in others. Again, feel free to use the various components for other dishes you create.

Ravioli

Combine the ricotta cheese, goat cheese, egg, Italian Seasonings and bread crumbs in a bowl and mix lightly. Lay the wontons out (3 per person) and place a tablespoon of the cheese mixture in the center of each one. Lightly brush the edges with water and fold over, making a triangle. Seal the edges with your fingers. Bring the 2 furthest corners together and join with a dab of water, forming what should look like a bishop's hat. Refrigerate until ready to use. These can also be frozen for several months and defrosted in the refrigerator for 24 hours before cooking.

Sundried Tomato Pesto

Place the sundried tomatoes, garlic, vinegar, pine nuts, cheese, olive oil, salt, lemon juice and red pepper flakes in a food processor and purée until smooth.

Mushrooms

Place the mushrooms in a sealable plastic bag. Add the olive oil, vinegar, garlic, salt and pepper, close the bag and remove as much of the air as possible. Seal the bag tightly and shake well to coat the mushrooms. Refrigerate overnight.

Assembly

Grill the mushrooms over a low flame for 6 minutes on one side and 5 minutes on the other. Boil the ravioli for 3 minutes. Drain the ravioli and place in a sauté pan with ¹/₄ cup of pesto per mushroom. Cook over medium-high heat until hot to the touch. Evenly divide the ravioli and sauce over each mushroom and top with a pinch of basil. Serve.

Leeks & Feta in Filo

One of the first chefs I worked for after graduating from the Culinary Institute of America was a brilliant and hilarious man by the name of Ed Snider. He taught me this simple and delicious recipe that makes a wonderful hors d'oeuvre. If you are unfamiliar with filo, it will take some getting used to. Don't give up if you get frustrated. The secret is in keeping it covered with a damp cloth when not working with it. When you are working with it, work quickly.

To *clean the leeks*, cut off the green top right above the white and discard the greens. Cut a slit in the leeks from just above the roots all the way to the top. Place under running water, fanning the leeks as you do to clean and rinse away all of the dirt. Slice the leeks thinly going towards the roots, stopping just short of them. Set aside.

Melt the butter in a medium-sized pot over medium-high heat. Add the leeks, salt, and pepper. Sauté for 5 minutes, stirring occasionally. Remove from the heat and stir in the garlic and dill. Cool for 20 to 30 minutes. Stir in the crumbled cheese.

Assembly

Thaw the filo according to the directions on the package. Unfold the filo and cover it with a damp cloth. Carefully pull a sheet of filo from the stack and place it on the work surface. Brush it with melted butter or spray it. Place another sheet on top and repeat the process until you have 3 sheets piled on top of each other. Next cut the pile in half lengthwise, making 2 columns.

Place about a tablespoon of the leek-feta mixture at the top and start rolling down. At about a quarter of the way down, fold in the sides and continue rolling (like a burrito). Place on a baking sheet lined with parchment and continue the process until all of the filling is used up.

Bake in a 400-degree oven for about 15 mintues or until golden brown. Serve hot or at room temperature.

Ingredients

3 leeks
4 tablespoons (1/2 stick) butter
1 teaspoon salt
1 teaspoon freshly ground black pepper
5 garlic cloves, minced
1 heaping tablespoon minced fresh dill
8 ounces feta cheese, crumbled
Filo dough
1/2 cup (1 stick) butter, melted, or butter-flavored cooking spray

Shrimp with Garlic & Vegetables

While relaxing in a hotel lounge in Santa Fe, New Mexico, enjoying a glass of Pinot Noir, and listening to the musicians, my mother, my brother, and I ordered some appetizers. One was this great shrimp dish that came in a rich broth and was served with crusty bread for dipping. We all fought over it, and when the bread was gone, I switched to a soup spoon to finish the last morsels. What follows is my own version of that delightfully simple snack. The garlic is a key element in this dish. Use caution not to burn it or your dish will be ruined.

Ingredients

15 garlic cloves, minced
1 tablespoon crushed red chile flakes
1/2 cup olive oil
1 zucchini, sliced
1 red bell pepper, diced
2 tomatoes, sliced
1/2 cup white wine
1 cup fish stock or clam juice
1 pound fresh shrimp, peeled and deveined
Juice of 2 limes
1/4 cup (packed) cilantro leaves
2 teaspoons salt
French baguette

Sauté the garlic and chile flakes in the olive oil for 5 minutes over low heat. Add the zucchini and bell pepper and sauté for 5 minutes. Add the tomatoes and cook for 2 more minutes. Pour in the wine and continue cooking for 5 minutes. Add the fish stock and bring to a boil. Once it has boiled add the shrimp and cook for 2 minutes. Remove from the heat. Squeeze in the lime juice and add the cilantro and salt. Serve immediately with crusty French bread.

Roasted Garlic Flan with Spiced Pecans

Very few people dislike garlic, especially roasted garlic. Here you'll enjoy it in a savory custard topped with delicious pecans. This flan can be served surrounded by my Southwest Mixed Green Salad with Cumin Vinaigrette (page 58)—omitting the pumpkin seeds and cheese—for a brilliant lunch entrée.

(page 58)

SERVES SIX

Flan

Place the cream in a microwave and heat just until it starts to boil. Put the eggs, egg yolks, sugar, cream cheese and roasted garlic in a blender. Pour in the scalded cream and pulse just until combined. Taste and add the salt, pepper and lemon juice.

Butter six 4-ounce ramekins and fill with cream mixture. Place the ramekins in a baking pan and pour hot water in the pan to reach halfway up the sides of the ramekins. Cover and bake at 325 degrees for about 35 minutes or until set.

Let cool overnight in the refrigerator before unmolding. Serve topped with Spiced Pecans.

Roasted Garlic

Cut the top off the head of garlic. Place in foil and top with the butter, wrap and roast in a 375-degree oven for 1 1/4 hours. When cool enough to handle, squeeze the garlic out of the skin.

Spiced Pecans

Melt the butter in an ovenproof sauté pan over medium heat. Stir in the honey. Add the Worcestershire sauce, pepper sauce, salt and pecans and stir to coat well. Place in a 350-degree oven for 10 minutes (check after 5 minutes as you don't want the nuts to burn).

Remove from the oven and allow to cool for 10 to 15 minutes. Spoon out with a slotted spoon, leaving the extra liquid (if any) in the pan.

Flan

1 1/2 cups heavy cream
2 eggs
2 egg yolks
2 teaspoons sugar
3 ounces cream cheese, softened
1 head garlic, roasted
Spiced Pecans in sauce
1 teaspoon salt
1 teaspoon white pepper
Juice of 1 lemon

Roasted Garlic

1 head garlic
2 tablespoons butter

Spiced Pecans

1 tablespoon butter
2 tablespoons honey
1 teaspoon Worcestershire sauce
1 teaspoon hot red pepper sauce
Pinch of salt
1 cup chopped pecans

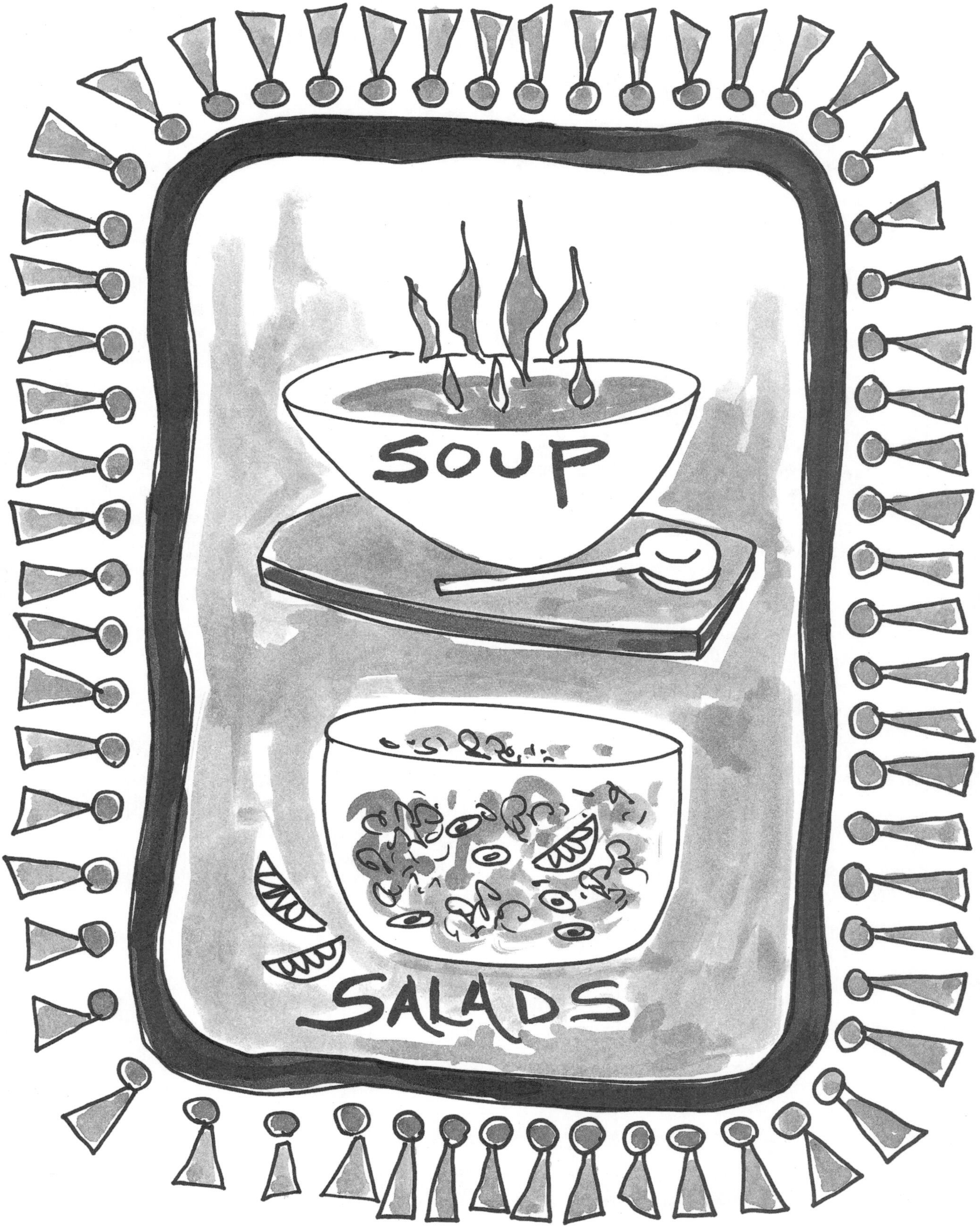
SOUP
SALADS

Since I like soups but don't eat them often, and I really don't make them at home very much, my only chance to enjoy them is when I am dining out. But then, as I mentioned in the previous chapter, my concentration is on what appetizer(s) I'm going to order. Usually what happens is that when I go out to dinner with my father or brother, both of whom love soup, I try to influence their decisions so that I can get a spoonful (or two, if it's my little brother)! I think that the other reason I don't make soups very often is that the majority of really superb soups depend on an excellent stock for the base. While I make very good stocks, I find it a little more difficult, not to mention more time-consuming, to make them at home. It is easier in a restaurant kitchen because different varieties of bones are readily available or only a phone call and delivery away.

The soup recipes that follow, therefore, are quite delicious, but they do not rely on labor-intensive, homemade stocks. They get their flavor from everything simmering in one pot or from heavy cream and butter. When making a soup, you can never go wrong using heavy cream or a béchamel sauce as the base. As a matter of fact, some of the best soups I have ever made are a result of emptying out my refrigerator into a pot, adding heavy cream, and puréeing it. Of course, when you use this approach to making soups, you do need some sort of organizing principle since salsa and leftover pudding would probably not make a great soup.

When it comes to salads, we have many choices: leafy greens, pasta, vegetables, rice, and protein (i.e., meat, fish, or chicken). One of my favorite things about salads is the dressing. I love making dressings, no matter what type of salad I am preparing. I think it has to do with the fact that I am the "King of the Robot Coupe" (a.k.a. a food processor)! If it can be made in the food processor, I do it. I can't resist throwing ingredients into the machine and creating a delicious emulsion. As a result of this Robot Coupe "emulsion compulsion," I have many unidentifiable sauces in my refrigerator.

In my opinion, lettuce is just a vehicle for the dressing, which means you need to create an absolutely fabulous "sauce." Any salad is a great way to have fun with flavors and ingredients. Pasta salads are fun, enjoyable, and always receive high praises. After all, who doesn't like pasta salad? They, just like protein salads, are only a matter of tossing a few ingredients in a bowl with a yummy dressing. What can be easier? The key to remember, though, when making a meat or pasta salad, is to allow time for the ingredients to marinate and absorb the dressing, preferably overnight.

I have no doubt that you will enjoy the recipes in this chapter for SOUPS AND SALADS as much as I do. The hardest thing about them is gathering the ingredients. A little secret for making non-leafy salads go further . . . put them on top of leaves. This works especially well if you turn something like my Rosemary Chicken Salad into a lunch entrée.

Salads · Soups

Greek Cucumber Salad	49
Orzo Salad	50
Simple Arugula Salad	50
Eggplant Salad	51
Rosemary Chicken Salad	51
Romaine, Avocado & Crab with Green Goddess	52
Ziti Pasta Salad	52
Caesar Tower with Parmesan Crisps & Worcestershire Oil	53
Spinach & Fried Oysters with Pernod Dressing	54
"Asian" Rice Noodle Salad with Sambal Shrimp	55
Cilantro Slaw	56
Spinach Salad with Italian Sausage Sherry Vinaigrette	57
Smoked Salmon Salad with Creamy Caper Dressing	58
Southwest Mixed Green Salad with Cumin Vinaigrette	58
Fresh Grilled Tuna & Artichoke Salad	59
Mushroom Brie Soup	60
Three-Cheese Soup with Basil Cream	61
Vermicelli Soup (Sopa de Fideo)	62
Creamy Tomato, Onion & Garlic Soup	62
Tortellini Soup	63
Beef Vegetable Soup	64
Asian-Style Noodle Soup	65
Tomato Garlic Soup with Saffron Rice	65

Greek Cucumber Salad

The first time I ever tasted feta cheese was on a Greek cucumber salad. It was in Albuquerque, New Mexico, at the home of Ray and Helen Comer (lovingly referred to as Tio and Tia). I've been addicted to it ever since (feta and Greek salad). One taste and you'll understand why. This salad is easy to prepare, requires no marination time, and is as fresh and refreshing as the vegetables you use. Serve it alongside my Spanakopita (page 27) from the previous chapter.

Cut the ends off the cucumber(s). Depending on your taste, either totally peel the cucumber, leave the skin on or, using a zester, zest the cucumber, leaving stripes of the peel. Cut the cucumber in half lengthwise. (If using regular cucumbers, seed them.) Slice the cucumber into 1/2- to 1/4-inch slices. Place the cucumber slices in a large bowl.

Cut the tomatoes in half and add them to the bowl along with the cheese and red onion.

Coarsely chop the olives and add them to the bowl.

Add the garlic, lemon juice, oregano, olive oils, salt and pepper. Gently toss and serve within 2 hours.

This salad may be made the day before and refrigerated, but must sit at room temperature for at least 2 hours and be tossed before serving.

Ingredients

1 English cucumber or 2 regular cucumbers

1 pint cherry or grape tomatoes or 10 ounces chopped tomatoes

1/2 cup crumbled feta cheese

1/3 cup julienned red onion

1 cup kalamata olives

3 garlic cloves, crushed

1/3 cup fresh lemon juice

1 tablespoon dried Mediterranean oregano

1/2 cup olive oil

2 tablespoons extra-virgin olive oil

1 teaspoon kosher salt

2 teaspoons freshly ground black pepper

Orzo Salad

Orzo is a small cut of pasta that looks almost like fat rice. Here it is used to make one of my favorite pasta salads. I recommend making it the day before you plan to serve it, so all the flavors have time to develop and mesh with the orzo.

Serves Five to Six

Ingredients

1 pound orzo

6 ounces feta cheese, crumbled

3/4 cup sliced kalamata olives

1/3 cup diced red onion

1/2 pint cherry or grape tomatoes, cut into halves

1/3 ounce fresh basil leaves, julienned (about 25 leaves)

3 garlic cloves

1/2 cup balsamic vinegar

1/4 cup apple cider vinegar

1 tablespoon Dijon mustard

1 tablespoon honey

Juice of 1 lemon

1/3 ounce fresh mint leaves (about 25 leaves)

Leaves of 1 (6-inch) sprig of rosemary

1 teaspoon salt

1 teaspoon freshly ground black pepper

1 2/3 cups olive oil

Cook the orzo according to the directions on the package. When the orzo is done, drain it and run cold water over it until it is cool; drain well. Place the orzo in a large bowl and add the feta cheese, olives, onion, tomatoes and basil. Set aside.

Place the garlic, vinegars, Dijon mustard, honey, lemon juice, mint leaves, rosemary leaves, salt and pepper in a food processor or blender and purée. Add the olive oil slowly to form an emulsion. Taste and adjust seasonings with salt and pepper if necessary. Pour the mixture over the orzo and toss well. Refrigerate for 4 to 8 hours before serving.

Simple Arugula Salad

It took me a while to acquire a taste for arugula. My first encounter with it was at Bayona, the restaurant where I worked in New Orleans. The chef, Susan Spicer, would toss it in with the romaine lettuce for her Caesar salad. I have since come to enjoy its flavor. This is a charming and simple salad with fresh, bold flavors.

Serves One

Ingredients

Large handful arugula

1/4 Preserved Lemon (page 115)

1/2 teaspoon Preserved Lemon liquid

Extra-virgin olive oil

Freshly ground black pepper

1 tablespoon pine nuts, toasted

Large pinch of goat cheese

Remove the stems from the arugula and discard them. Remove the lemon pulp and dice the rind. Place the arugula, Preserved Lemon and lemon liquid in a bowl. Lightly drizzle with the olive oil. Season with pepper and toss. Serve topped with the pine nuts and goat cheese. Multiply as many times as needed.

Eggplant Salad

You'll notice that eggplant is used quite often in this book—it's my favorite vegetable. It's funny that I like it so much because my father won't touch it. He says it's what they used to feed the pigs when he was growing up. Apparently he relates it to "pig slop." Little does he know that I have added eggplant to many a dish that he has thoroughly enjoyed—and asked for seconds! This light, refreshing salad is great on a hot day with a glass of New Zealand Sauvignon Blanc.

Coat the eggplant and poblano chile with the olive oil and place on a baking sheet. Roast in a 350-degree oven for 1 hour. Cool for 1 hour.

Place the eggplant and chile in a food processor with the yogurt and garlic. Pulse a few times to create a chunky purée. Transfer the mixture to a bowl.

Quarter the tomatoes; cut out the centers and discard. Dice the tomatoes. Add the tomatoes and the olives to the bowl. Thinly slice the tops of the green onions and add to the bowl. Stir and season with the salt and pepper. Refrigerate until ready to serve.

SERVES FOUR

Ingredients
1 eggplant, peeled
1 poblano chile, seeded
3 tablespoons extra-virgin olive oil
2/3 cup plain yogurt
2 garlic cloves
2 tomatoes
1/2 cup sliced green olives
Tops of 1 bunch green onions
1 teaspoon each salt and pepper

Chef's Note
Serve with crackers, pita bread, in sandwiches, or in lettuce cups. You can even garnish with roasted peppers or pine nuts.

Rosemary Chicken Salad

There is a little more work involved in the making of this chicken salad than in that of others. The outcome, however, is well worth it. My favorite way to enjoy this salad is atop a large bed of mixed greens.

Combine the olive oil, paprika, sugar, garlic, balsamic vinegar, 2 teaspoons kosher salt, pepper and rosemary. Toss the mixture with the chicken and place in a baking pan. Bake in a 350-degree oven for 35 to 45 minutes. Cool completely.

Cut the chicken into 1/4-inch pieces. Toss the chicken with the mayonnaise, red onion, vinegar, 1 teaspoon kosher salt, honey and Dijon mustard. Taste and adjust seasonings.

Refrigerate for 8 to 12 hours.

SERVES SIX TO EIGHT

Ingredients
2/3 cup olive oil
1 teaspoon paprika
1 tablespoon sugar
4 garlic cloves, minced
1/4 cup balsamic vinegar
2 teaspoons kosher salt
1 teaspoon pepper
1/4 cup minced fresh rosemary
3 pounds boneless skinless
   chicken breasts
1 cup mayonnaise
1 red onion, diced
1 tablespoon cider vinegar
1 teaspoon kosher salt
1 tablespoon honey
1 tablespoon Dijon mustard

Romaine, Avocado & Crab with Green Goddess

SERVES FIVE TO SEVEN

Green Goddess Dressing
1 ounce anchovy fillets, drained
1 bunch green onions
1 bunch parsley
5 garlic cloves
1/3 cup tarragon vinegar
1 quart mayonnaise

Salad
3 romaine hearts, torn
3 avocados, peeled and diced
1 1/2 to 2 cups crab meat, flaked

Green goddess dressing brings back fond memories of dinnertime with the family—fresh lettuce, juicy tomatoes, crisp cucumbers, and ripe avocados slathered with this rich and creamy dressing. A little hint for dressing a salad is to toss it right before you serve it instead of putting the cruet on the table and allowing each person to pour their own. You'll use less dressing. My Green Goddess Dressing recipe makes a lot, but it is full of flavor and you'll be glad you have extra.

Green Goddess Dressing
Purée the anchovy fillets, green onions, parsley, garlic and vinegar in a food processor until smooth. Add the mayonnaise and pulse until mixed. Refrigerate.

Salad
Toss the romaine, avocados, and crab meat with enough Dressing to coat. Extra Dressing will remain safe in the refrigerator for many months.

Ziti Pasta Salad

SERVES SIX TO EIGHT

Ingredients
1 pound ziti
1/3 cup olive oil
1/3 cup balsamic vinegar
1 (14 1/2-ounce) can diced tomatoes
4 garlic cloves
5 anchovy fillets
2 (2/3-ounce) bunches fresh basil
1 cup kalamata olives, coarsely chopped
2 Roma tomatoes, cut into eighths
1/2 cup grated Parmesan cheese
1 teaspoon kosher salt
1 tablespoon freshly ground black pepper
1 tablespoon crushed red pepper flakes

The idea and base for this pasta salad comes from a recipe entitled "Joe's Favorite Pasta Salad" by my friend Lynn Nicklo. The "Joe" in the title refers to her husband—my brother Tommy's fishing buddy. Both Lynn and Joe are great cooks. As a matter of fact, if you are a garlic lover I suggest checking out Lynn's web site at www.4garlic.com (I highly recommend any item you find there). The original recipe was a little simpler. I, of course, had to throw my chef's spin on it. What I like most, besides the taste, is that there really isn't much fat in it. Again, allow the salad to rest overnight for maximum flavor.

Cook the ziti according to package instructions. Drain the pasta and set aside to cool.

Purée the olive oil, balsamic vinegar, canned tomatoes (with juice), garlic cloves, anchovies, and 1 bunch of the basil in a blender or Robot Coupe. Pour over the chilled pasta.

Thinly slice the remaining basil leaves and add to the pasta along with the kalamata olives, tomatoes, cheese, salt, pepper and pepper flakes. Toss well. Adjust seasonings if necessary.

Refrigerate for 8 hours to overnight.

Caesar Tower with Parmesan Crisps & Worcestershire Oil

This salad is probably better suited for special occasions. It is pretty and makes an impressive presentation. The last time I served it to company, I think they enjoyed the crisps more than they did the greens—especially Mrs. Eileen (John) Daniels, who hounded me for months for the Parmesan Crisp recipe. I must admit that they are quite addictive and can be used for a multitude of things besides this salad. When making them, always bake more than you need so that you do not eat up what you planned to serve to your guests. Fortunately for Mrs. Daniels, I wrote this cookbook; otherwise, she may never have gotten the recipe!

Parmesan Crisps

Line a baking sheet with a Silpat. Sprinkle 2 teaspoons of the cheese in a corner of the Silpat and spread into a 2-inch circle with your fingertips. Repeat until you have 12 circles, equally spaced. Bake in a 325-degree oven for 8 to 10 minutes or until golden brown. Using a small spatula, transfer the crisps to a paper towel. They will be soft at first but will harden as they cool. Store in an airtight container for no more than 2 days. Repeat the process, making 12 more crisps.

Caesar Dressing

In the bowl of a food processor, place the pepper sauce, garlic cloves, anchovy fillets, lemon juice, Dijon mustard, egg yolks, salt and vinegar. Purée until smooth. With motor running, slowly add the olive oils in a thin stream, forming an emulsion. (If adding Parmesan cheese, do so after forming an emulsion.) Refrigerate until ready.

Worcestershire Oil

Combine the Worcestershire sauce and olive oil and set aside until ready to use.

Assembly

Toss the romaine with just enough Dressing to coat. Place a Crisp in the center of each plate and top with a small handful of the tossed romaine. Top the romaine with another Crisp and then more romaine. Finish with the remaining Crisps and drizzle the Worcestershire Oil around the tower. Serve immediately.

SERVES EIGHT

Parmesan Crisps

1 cup finely grated Parmigiano-Reggiano cheese

Caesar Dressing

1 teaspoon hot red pepper sauce
4 garlic cloves
5 anchovy fillets
1/4 cup fresh lemon juice
1 tablespoon Dijon mustard
2 egg yolks
1/2 teaspoon salt
1/4 cup red wine vinegar
2 tablespoons extra-virgin olive oil
1 3/4 cups olive oil
1 cup grated Parmesan cheese (optional)

Worcestershire Oil

2 tablespoons Worcestershire sauce
3 tablespoons extra-virgin olive oil

Assembly

3 romaine hearts, thinly sliced
Caesar Dressing
24 Parmesan Crisps
Worcestershire Oil

Spinach & Fried Oysters with Pernod Dressing

If you like fried oysters, here's a great way to eat them. Enjoy this salad as an entrée or divide it into smaller portions for a course at a dinner party.

YIELDS FOUR LARGE SALADS

Pernod Dressing
1 egg
1 egg yolk
3 garlic cloves
2 tablespoons fresh lemon juice
1 teaspoon salt
1 teaspoon hot red pepper sauce
2 tablespoons Pernod
1 cup olive oil
4 green onions, sliced
1 tablespoon chopped fresh dill
1/2 cup buttermilk

Spinach Salad
Fresh spinach leaves, cleaned
    and stemmed, thinly sliced
3 carrots, julienned
1/2 celery root, julienned

Fried Oysters
1 cup masa harina
2 tablespoons Cajun seasoning
2 eggs
1 cup buttermilk
2 cups panko (Japanese bread
    crumbs)
Oil for frying
24 large oysters, drained
Toasted Pecans

Chef's Note
I prefer Maseca brand masa harina, but the important distinction is in using corn-based masa, not masa trigo, which is flour-based.

Pernod Dressing
Place the eggs, garlic, lemon juice, salt, pepper sauce, and Pernod in a blender or a food processor. Purée for about a minute. With the motor still running, slowly pour in the olive oil until an emulsion has been formed. Pour into a bowl and stir in the green onions and dill. Slowly whisk in the buttermilk. Store in the refrigerator until needed.

Spinach Salad
In a large bowl, combine the spinach, julienne of carrots and celery root. Cover with a damp towel and keep in the refrigerator until ready to serve.

Fried Oysters
In a shallow bowl, combine the masa harina and Cajun seasonings. In another shallow dish, whisk together the eggs and buttermilk. Place the bread crumbs in a third shallow dish.

Pour about 1/4 inch of oil in a skillet and heat on high. It's hot enough when the oil "sizzles" when you drop some bread crumbs in it. Carefully place the oysters in the hot oil (do not overcrowd) and cook on each side for about 1 1/2 minutes. Drain on paper towels and sprinkle with salt.

Assembly
Toss the spinach mix and pecans with as much Dressing as desired. Mound the salad in the center of each plate. Arrange 5 oysters around the salad and 1 on top. Sprinkle Cajun seasoning (I like to use Zydeco Zest) all over the plate and serve immediately.

"Asian" Rice Noodle Salad with Sambal Shrimp

This is a basic cold spring roll/summer roll without the roll.
I invented it one day when I had no rice paper and was too lazy to drive to the local (which I must say is not too local) Oriental market. For once, something good came out of my laziness! Here again I will say, add or delete ingredients to your liking. You may even want to substitute tofu, chicken, or pork for the shrimp. In any case, make it yours. As in the spring roll recipe in the previous chapter, I recommend that you do not delete the basil, mint, or cilantro. It's great for a buffet, but remember to toss with the dressing right before your party starts.

Sambal Oelek Vinaigrette & Shrimp

Place the lime juice, Maggi seasoning, sesame oil, peanut oil, soy sauce, sugar, garlic, fish sauce, sambal oelek, vinegar and ginger in a blender and purée until smooth. Put the shrimp in a bowl and pour the vinaigrette over them. Marinate in the refrigerator for 2 hours to overnight.

Salad

Prepare the cucumber by cutting off the ends, cutting in half lengthwise and slicing 1/4 inch thick. (If using regular cucumbers, cut in half and scoop out and discard the seeds before slicing.) Place the rice sticks on the bottom of a big serving dish. Top with the cabbage and bean sprouts. Add carrots and cucumber. Top with the radishes, green onions and peppers.

Spoon the marinated shrimp (along with the desired amount of dressing) over the top and sprinkle with all of the herbs.

Garnish with the chopped peanuts.

SERVES EIGHT TO TEN

Sambal Oelek Vinaigrette & Shrimp

1 cup fresh lime juice
10 to 20 splashes Maggi seasoning
1/4 cup sesame oil
1/2 cup peanut oil
1/4 cup soy sauce
1/2 cup sugar
5 garlic cloves
1 tablespoon fish sauce
2 tablespoons sambal oelek
1/4 cup rice vinegar
1 1/2-inch piece fresh ginger, grated
12 ounces peeled cooked shrimp

Salad

1 English (hothouse) cucumber or 2 regular cucumbers
1 pound rice sticks, cooked
1 large head napa or savoy cabbage, julienned
1 handful bean sprouts
1 cup (about) carrots, julienned
1 bunch radishes, julienned
1 bunch green onions, cut on the bias
1 red bell pepper, julienned
Shrimp in Sambal Oelek Vinaigrette
1 bunch each (approximately 2/3 ounce) mint, basil and cilantro
1/2 cup chopped peanuts

Cilantro Slaw

This is a nice, light coleslaw that gets its flavor from cilantro.
If you can find sweet or candied jalapeños, they make a great addition.
The original recipe, which I have since changed, was shared with me by
April Smith, a friend of my mother. In her version, which she called
Dry Slaw, the vegetables were mixed and served separately from the
dressing; everyone was to pour it onto their individual portion.
It's a good idea if you have a group of people that are counting calories.
Otherwise, toss the whole thing together right before serving.
This recipe may be cut in half with NO problem.

Salad

2 bunches cilantro
1 head red cabbage, thinly sliced
1 head green cabbage, thinly sliced
2 heads butter lettuce (Boston or Bibb), torn
2 cups shredded carrots
1 to 2 cups candied jalapeño chile slices, drained (optional)

Dressing

6 to 8 garlic cloves
1 1/2 tablespoons (about) salt
2 to 3 teaspoons coarsely ground black pepper
1 teaspoon dry mustard
2/3 cup rice vinegar
2 cups olive oil
Cilantro stems (from above)

Salad

Remove the cilantro leaves from the stems and reserve the stems for the Dressing. Coarsely chop the cilantro leaves. Toss the red and green cabbage, butter lettuce, carrots, cilantro and candied jalapeño chile together and set aside.

Dressing

Place the garlic, salt, pepper, dry mustard, rice vinegar, olive oil and cilantro stems in a blender and purée until smooth. Taste seasonings and adjust if necessary.

Spinach Salad with Italian Sausage Sherry Vinaigrette

My favorite way to eat spinach salad is when it is tossed with a warm dressing. Here I use Italian sausage, but you can use any other type of sausage if you prefer. Remember, though, that you must start out with it in the raw stage in order to achieve maximum flavor. The fat you are rendering contributes to much of the taste. One thing to keep in mind when making hot vinaigrettes is that an acid, like vinegar, evaporates fast. You will need to taste this dressing before you serve it to make sure that the acidic balance is still there. If not, add a splash or two of the vinegar before serving in order to achieve the flavor you like.

Rinse and dry the spinach. Remove the stems and julienne. Set aside.

Cook the sausage in a sauce pot. When almost ready, add the minced shallots and continue cooking, being careful not to burn the shallots. Deglaze the pot with the orange juice and continue cooking for about 3 minutes. Stir in the Dijon mustard and vinegar. Slowly whisk in the olive oil.

Taste and adjust seasonings. If you find it too tart, add more olive oil; if not tart enough, add a splash or two of vinegar. Serve warm, tossed with the spinach.

SERVES SIX

Ingredients

8 cups (about) spinach leaves

1/2 pound Italian sausage, casings removed

2 shallots, minced

1/4 cup fresh orange juice

3 tablespoons Dijon mustard

1/2 cup sherry vinegar

1 cup olive oil

1 teaspoon freshly ground black pepper

1 teaspoon salt

Smoked Salmon Salad with Creamy Caper Dressing

Ingredients

2 tablespoons butter
1 red onion, cut into halves
    and sliced
Several sprigs fresh dill
2/3 cup capers
1 pound cream cheese, softened
1/4 cup fresh lemon juice
1 tablespoon black pepper
2 cups olive oil
6 to 8 cups torn butter lettuce
    (Boston or Bibb)
1 pound smoked salmon
2 hard-cooked eggs, chopped

For those of you that like bagels and lox with all of the traditional accompaniments, this is the salad for you. The dressing is quite unique and very rich. I created this salad as a way to use up scraps of smoked salmon. You can do the same as long as the scraps are from a good piece of fish.

Melt the butter in a sauté pan over high heat. Add the onion and cook until soft and the onion starts to brown. Place the onion, dill, capers, cream cheese, lemon juice and pepper in a food processor and purée. Slowly add the olive oil. Taste and season. Refrigerate until ready to serve.

Assembly

Divide the lettuce among the plates and top with equal portions of the salmon. Drizzle with the dressing and sprinkle with the chopped eggs. Feel free to garnish with any of your favorite vegetables (such as tomatoes, bell peppers, squash).

Southwest Mixed Green Salad with Cumin Vinaigrette

Cumin Vinaigrette

1/2 cup balsamic vinegar
1 tablespoon honey
1 tablespoon Dijon mustard
1 tablespoon lemon juice
1/3 cup cumin
1 teaspoon each salt and pepper
1 shallot
3 garlic cloves
1 1/2 cups olive oil

Salad

6 cups (about) mixed field greens
Handful of cilantro leaves
1/2 cup toasted pumpkin seeds
4 to 6 ounces queso fresco or
    feta cheese, crumbled

If you like the flavors of the Southwest, you will certainly enjoy them as they come together in this salad. Don't save the dressing for this green dish alone. Try it as a marinade for any meat, seafood, or poultry.

Cumin Vinaigrette

Purée the balsamic vinegar, honey, Dijon mustard, lemon juice, cumin, salt, pepper, shallot and garlic in a food processor, blender or Robot Coupe. Slowly add the oil. Taste and adjust the seasonings. Refrigerate.

Assembly

Toss the greens, cilantro, pumpkin seeds and cheese together. Drizzle with the desired amount of Vinaigrette and toss.

Fresh Grilled Tuna & Artichoke Salad

Tuna salad doesn't have to come from a can. For this delicacy, fresh tuna is grilled and combined with artichokes and blended with homemade mayonnaise. If you are an expert with fresh artichokes, feel free to use them instead—prepared ones are just a little easier. Once you try this version, you'll be kicking the can!

Tuna Salad

Make sure that the tuna is cut into steaks or pieces that are no more than 1 inch thick. Rub the tuna with the olive oil and sprinkle 1 side with salt and pepper. Place the tuna, seasoned side down, on a very hot grill and season the exposed side. Cook for 5 minutes and then turn over, cooking for another 5 minutes. Remove from heat and allow to cool.

Crumble the tuna into a bowl. Add the chopped artichoke hearts and the desired amount of Mayonnaise. Mix well, taste and adjust the seasonings (if necessary) with salt and freshly ground black pepper. Refrigerate for 4 to 12 hours before serving.

Homemade Mayonnaise

To coddle the eggs, carefully drop them in boiling water for 2 minutes. Cool by running cold water over them. Carefully crack them open and scoop out the insides.

Place the coddled eggs, water, vinegar, lime juice, mustard, salt and pepper sauce in a food processor (or in a bowl if you prefer to whisk by hand) and combine until light and fluffy. Add the oil slowly until an emulsion has been formed. Taste and adjust seasonings if necessary. Refrigerate.

Tuna Salad

1 1/2 pounds fresh tuna
Extra-virgin olive oil
Kosher salt and freshly ground
    black pepper to taste
12 ounces marinated artichoke
    hearts, drained and chopped
Homemade Mayonnaise

Homemade Mayonnaise

2 eggs, coddled
1 tablespoon water
1 tablespoon apple cider vinegar
Juice of 1 lime
1 teaspoon prepared mustard
2 teaspoons kosher salt
1 teaspoon hot red pepper sauce
2 cups oil

Mushroom Brie Soup

In the previous chapter I mentioned a chef that I worked with named Ed Snider. Before working with Ed, I had met him when he was the Executive Chef at a private club my parents belong to. For a while it was tradition that my father took me there for lunch on my birthday. On one such occasion Ed served this incredible soup. When I asked him about it, he took out his business card and scribbled down the recipe. In doing research for this book, I came across that business card and knew that I had to include it. I never thought that years later I would be working for the man, and that when he left, I would take his place. I learned some good basics from Ed. I lost contact with him about six years ago, unfortunately. If you happen to know Chef Ed Snider, tell him I said hello and to call me.

Béchamel

1/4 cup (1/2 stick) butter
1 tablespoon finely chopped
    onion
1/4 cup flour
5 cups milk
Salt and white pepper to taste
Pinch of grated fresh nutmeg

Mushrooms

2 tablespoons butter
2 cups sliced fresh button
    mushrooms
1/2 teaspoon salt
1/2 teaspoon white pepper
2 cups cubed Brie
Juice of 1 lemon

Béchamel

Melt 1/4 cup butter in a saucepan. Add the onion and cook until translucent. Add the flour and continue cooking over low heat, stirring frequently, for about 8 minutes. Be careful not to brown the onions or the flour. Pour the milk in slowly and whisk until well-incorporated. Simmer for 45 minutes or until thick, stirring frequently. Season with the salt, pepper and nutmeg to taste.

Mushrooms

Melt 2 tablespoons butter in a sauté pan over medium-high heat. Cook the mushrooms in the butter with 1/2 teaspoon each salt and white pepper until tender. Taste and adjust the seasonings. Place the mushrooms in a food processor and purée. Add to the Béchamel along with the Brie. Whisk until smooth.

Strain the soup through a cheesecloth into a clean pot. Add the lemon juice and adjust the salt if needed.

Three-Cheese Soup with Basil Cream

When I travel, I carry with me a little notebook in which I jot down food ideas after seeing them on a menu or eating them. While vacationing in San Miguel de Allende, Mexico, I made sure I always had that trusty little pad. I ran across the notebook when I first started brainstorming for this book. One entry I had scribbled down was "Cheese Soup with Basil Cream." To be honest, I have no recollection of what it tasted like, much less where I tasted it. It did, however (as it was intended to do), spark something in me to create this recipe.

Soup

Make a roux by melting the butter in a sauté pan; add the flour. Combine well and cook over medium-high heat for 2 minutes, stirring constantly.

Pour the cold milk into the pan and whisk. Add the nutmeg, salt, and pepper sauce. Bring the mixture to a boil. Reduce the heat and simmer for 30 minutes, stirring often and scraping the corners and bottom of the pan to prevent burning.

Add the wine and cheeses. Stir until well-combined. Add the lemon juice and serve topped with a dollop of Basil Cream.

Basil Cream

Place the basil and sour cream in a blender or Robot Coupe and pulse until well-combined. Refrigerate until serving.

Soup

1/2 cup (1 stick) butter
1/2 cup flour
1/2 gallon milk
1/4 teaspoon grated fresh nutmeg
2 teaspoons salt
2 teaspoons hot red pepper sauce (recommend Sriracha Hot Chile Sauce)
1/2 cup chardonnay
1/2 pound Gouda cheese, grated
1/2 pound Havarti cheese, grated
1/2 pound farmer cheese, grated
Juice of 1 lemon
Basil Cream

Basil Cream

2/3 ounce fresh basil
8 ounces sour cream

Vermicelli Soup (Sopa de Fideo)

SERVES FOUR

Ingredients

8 ounces vermicelli
2 tablespoons corn oil
6 garlic cloves, sliced
1 white onion, coarsely chopped
2 teaspoons salt
2 teaspoons cumin
1 tablespoon chile powder
1 fresh jalapeño chile, chopped
2 tomatoes, chopped
8 cups well-seasoned chicken stock
1 cup frozen peas
Cilantro (optional)

I grew up eating a thicker version of this recipe—more of a pasta than a soup—laced with tiny bits of meat. For me it has to be one of the ultimate Mexican comfort foods. Here I present it to you as a soup, also very popular in the Mexican culture.

Place the vermicelli, corn oil, garlic, onion, salt, cumin, chile powder and jalapeño chile in a pot and cook over medium-high heat for 3 to 5 minutes, stirring constantly until the vermicelli noodles have started to brown. Add the chopped tomatoes and stir. Add the stock and bring to a boil. Turn the heat down, cover and simmer for 15 minutes.

Stir in the peas. Taste and adjust the salt if necessary. Serve garnished with cilantro if desired.

Creamy Tomato, Onion & Garlic Soup

YIELDS FIVE CUPS (UNSTRAINED)

Ingredients

2 pounds (about 6 medium-sized) tomatoes
1 pound yellow onions
3 ounces garlic cloves, peeled
2 tablespoons extra-virgin olive oil
1 teaspoon salt
1 teaspoon freshly ground black pepper
16 ounces (1 pint) heavy cream
4 tablespoons (1/2 stick) butter
1 teaspoon hot red pepper sauce
Juice of 1 lemon
Herbs to garnish

Cream soups are probably my favorite types of soup . . . of course! This one is no exception. When presenting it I have no problem serving it unstrained. If you prefer a much smoother, more delicate soup, feel free to squeeze it through some cheesecloth.

Cut the tomatoes into quarters and scoop out the seeds. Place the tomatoes on a baking sheet. Peel the onions and cut them into 1-inch pieces. Add the onions and garlic to the baking sheet and toss with the olive oil, salt and pepper. Roast in a 350-degree oven for 45 minutes. Place the vegetables in a blender with the cream and purée.

At this point you may either strain the soup or leave it as is. Pour into a pot. Add the butter, pepper sauce and lemon juice and warm over medium heat. Taste and adjust seasonings, if necessary, with salt. Serve garnished with your favorite chopped herb(s).

Tortellini Soup

As you may have read by now, I was born in Albuquerque,
New Mexico, and lived there for not quite the first year of my life. My
parents had some good friends there that my brother and I affectionately
referred to as Tia and Tio (the Spanish words for aunt and uncle). Tia and
Tio really were our family. I have fond memories of being a young child and
flying to Albuquerque to visit them over the summer. They had a large
garden in their back yard and are probably the ones that introduced me to
homegrown vegetables. This soup is one that Tia used to make
using the fresh produce from her garden.

Brown the meat in a soup pot
with the onions, garlic, basil,
oregano, salt and pepper. Drain
off any extra fat. Add the broth,
wine, tomatoes, tomato sauce
and carrots. Bring to a boil.
Reduce heat; simmer uncovered
for 30 minutes.

Stir in the zucchini, tortellini
(if using frozen), parsley and
bell pepper. Cover and simmer
for 35 minutes or until tortellini
is tender. Taste and adjust the
seasonings.

If using fresh tortellini, add it
about 7 minutes before the soup
is done.

Ingredients

1 pound ground beef or Italian
  sausage, casings removed
1 cup chopped yellow onions
2 garlic cloves, minced
1 teaspoon dry basil
1 teaspoon dry oregano
1 teaspoon salt
1 teaspoon freshly ground
  black pepper
43 ounces beef broth
1/2 cup dry red wine
6 small tomatoes, cut into
  quarters and seeds removed
1 (8-ounce) can tomato sauce
1 cup thinly sliced carrots
1/2 cup sliced zucchini
2 cups fresh or frozen cheese
  tortellini
3 tablespoons chopped fresh
  Italian parsley
1 medium green bell pepper, cut
  into 1/2-inch slices

Beef Vegetable Soup

As I was writing this chapter on soups, I remembered a soup that my mother used to make on cold winter days. If you are familiar with South Texas weather, you will understand when I say that she didn't make it very often! When she did, however, we all devoured it. In my opinion, what makes this soup are the tomatoes and chiles you simmer in the broth to make a salsa that each person stirs into his or her bowl. When I sat down with my mother to write this recipe, she told me that both of my parents actually created it. My mother apparently used to make a vegetable soup, and my father, who is a meat-and-potatoes man, encouraged the addition of the meat, and, yes, the potatoes. My mother sometimes stirs rice or egg noodles into the pot during the last half hour or so before serving. I hope this soup warms your family's hearts the way it does ours.

Ingredients

1/4 cup corn oil

4 pounds beef shanks
   (about 4 to 6)

Salt to taste

Freshly ground black pepper
   to taste

5 ribs celery

1 yellow onion

1 pound carrots

1 cup tomato sauce

1 garlic bulb, peeled

1 gallon hot water

2 bay leaves

1 teaspoon each of your favorite
   herbs (fresh or dried)

1 head cabbage, coarsely
   chopped

3 potatoes (about 1 1/2 pounds),
   large dice

1 zucchini, sliced

1 yellow squash, sliced

5 to 7 tomatoes

1 to 3 jalapeño chiles to taste

2 teaspoons salt

Heat the corn oil in a large sauce pot until smoking. Season each side of the beef with salt and pepper to taste. Brown the beef shanks for 3 minutes on each side, removing each when browned on all sides. Turn the heat to low and sauté the celery, onion and carrots. Cook for 7 minutes, stirring occasionally. Stir in the tomato sauce and garlic. Cook for 5 minutes. Add the seared beef, water, bay leaves and seasonings of your choice. Bring to a boil. Cover and reduce the heat to simmer. Simmer for 2 hours.

Add the cabbage and potatoes and simmer for 1 hour.

Stir in the zucchini and squash. Place the tomatoes and jalapeño chiles on top, cover, and simmer for 1 more hour. Turn off the heat.

Remove the jalapeño chiles and tomatoes. Cool. Skin the tomatoes and discard the jalapeño pepper stems. Place in a blender with 2 teaspoons salt. Pulse until combined. Set aside. Serve bowls of soup topped with this salsa.

Asian-Style Noodle Soup

Of all the soups in this book, this one is by far the easiest. It smacks the palate—literally—as you slurp up the noodles. You may only want to make this soup for you and your family to enjoy; it can get quite messy drawing in the noodles. But don't let etiquette stop you from enjoying this flavorful soup. I'll tell you that I know of no simple way to eat it (unless you cut the noodles into small pieces, and then what fun is there in that). So tuck a napkin(s) into your shirt and slurp away. You won't be sorry you did.

Place the broth, fish sauce, lime juice, soy sauce, vinegar and lemon grass in a sauce pot and bring to a boil. Cover and continue boiling for 2 minutes.

Remove the lemon grass and add the noodles. Cook until soft, about 5 minutes. Thinly slice the chile and tops of the green onions (stop at the white part).

Chop the cilantro coarsely. Remove the sauce pot from the heat and stir in the cilantro, chile and onions. Serve immediately.

You can add anything you want to this soup, such as cooked shrimp, chicken, beef or pork or even fresh or canned mushrooms.

SERVES FOUR TO SIX

Ingredients

2 quarts beef, chicken, vegetable or seafood broth (homemade or store-bought)

1/4 cup fish sauce

1/4 cup fresh lime juice

1 tablespoon soy sauce

1 tablespoon white vinegar

1 (3-inch) piece lemon grass, sliced into 1/4-inch pieces

4 ounces soba noodles or rice sticks

1 serrano or Thai chile

1 bunch green onions

1 bunch cilantro

Tomato Garlic Soup with Saffron Rice

This was my "House Soup" for a while at a restaurant where I worked. Don't be fooled by its simplicity. It has a nice flavor and is always met with rave reviews. The secret is allowing it plenty of time to simmer so that the flavors can develop. I have not included a recipe for the saffron rice. It's easily made by adding some strands of saffron to a basic rice recipe. Alternatively, I suggest Mahatma® brand saffron rice, which is readily available at your grocery store.

Drain the tomatoes, reserving the juice. Crush the tomatoes with your hand. Warm the olive oil and garlic in a sauce pot over medium-low heat. Cook the oil until it has reached a golden color. (Do not burn!) Add the tomatoes, bay leaf, cumin and paprika, and sauté for 10 minutes, stirring occasionally.

Pour in the reserved tomato juice and water. Season with the salt and pepper. Bring to a boil. Reduce the heat and simmer for at least 50 minutes. Blend in lemon juice. Taste and adjust the seasonings. Discard the bay leaf. Serve topped with about 1/2 cup saffron rice.

SERVES EIGHT TO TEN

Ingredients

1 (28-ounce) can whole tomatoes

3 tablespoons olive oil

1 cup slivered garlic

1 bay leaf

1 tablespoon cumin

1/2 cup paprika

7 cups water

1 teaspoon salt

1 teaspoon freshly ground black pepper

4 cups (about) cooked saffron rice

Juice of 1 lemon

*A*lthough I had some great Italian teachers (here I mean heritage, not classes) at the Culinary Institute of America, I never fully understood Italian cooking, more specifically pasta, until I met Sue Leone and Joe Saglimbeni. Both of them are die-hard Italians and excellent cooks.

Please understand that I know (and hopefully you do too) that Italian cooking involves much more than pasta. It's just that I am fascinated by it. There are 101 cuts of pasta and 1,001 different sauces and preparations. The possibilities and combinations are endless. You can use pasta for a base to create any dish you want, from an hors d'oeuvre to dessert and everything in between.

If you are reading through this book in chronological order, you know by now my love for fat—heavy cream and butter in particular. When it comes to pasta, however, that is not the case. I could eat spaghetti with tomato sauce— or should I say pasta with red sauce, which covers the whole gamut—every day. The flavors I am looking for come from good olive oils, nuts, and cheeses. Nonetheless, several recipes in these pages of pasta do call for heavy cream and butter. I couldn't go cold turkey, you know!

The recipes that you will encounter in these upcoming pages are really quite "to die for," as my brother Tommy says. For the most part, they are simple and uncomplicated, which describes the bulk of pasta cooking. When at all possible, use very fresh tomatoes—sniff them for that fresh vine smell. Buy tomatoes three to four days before you plan to use them, making certain they have turned red and feel tender. Never refrigerate a tomato unless you suddenly find it has ripened too long. Finally, if you are unsure about the freshness and/or taste of a tomato, it is perfectly acceptable to use canned. One of my favorite choices is Cento® brand, chef's cut. This is a really good canned tomato.

So there you have it, my thoughts on PASTA.
They are all delectable and can be served as an appetizer,
pasta, or main course. Mangia Bene!

Pasta

Linguine with Red Clam Sauce

I was never a big fan of fish-based sauces with pasta until I did some experimenting in the kitchen. I really like this pasta dish. It is neither too heavy nor very fishy tasting. I suggest serving it in big bowls with a good loaf of bread to help absorb the nice sauce left in the bowl. Although this is a red sauce, a nice glass of white wine will go great with it.

Prepare the pasta using the package directions. Drain and toss with the extra-virgin olive oil. Set aside.

Heat 1/4 cup olive oil in a sauté pan. Add the garlic, chile flakes and Italian Seasonings. Sauté for 1 minute. Add the clams and cook for another minute. Pour in the wine and clam juice. Add the tomatoes and salt.

Remove from the heat and stir in the parsley.

To serve, top the linguine with the sauce and cheese.

SERVES FOUR TO SIX

Ingredients

1 pound linguine
1/4 cup (about) extra-virgin olive oil
1/4 cup olive oil
6 garlic cloves, minced
1 tablespoon red chile flakes
1 tablespoon Italian Seasonings (page 74)
1 (10-ounce) can baby clams, drained
2/3 cup white wine
1/2 cup clam juice
1 (28-ounce) can chopped tomatoes
Kosher salt to taste
1 bunch Italian parsley, chopped
Grated Parmesan cheese

Seared Sea Scallops over Fettuccine

When you read the ingredients, you will see that this pasta has an incredibly rich sauce—probably the richest I have ever tasted, not to mention the best. It's easy to prepare. If you are not a scallops fan, like I am, try it with shrimp, salmon, or even chicken. If you are concerned that it may be too rich, I suggest eating it once a year as an appetizer. It is so good you really can't pass it up.

Prepare the pasta using the package directions. Set aside. Heat the Boursin, cream, lemon juice and 1 teaspoon salt over medium heat, stirring occasionally until the cheese is melted. Turn the heat to low until ready to use. Heat a large sauté pan over a high flame. Toss the scallops and 1/4 cup olive oil in a bowl with 1 teaspoon salt and pepper.

Place 2 tablespoons olive oil in the sauté pan and heat to smoking. Place the scallops in the pan flat side down and cook for 3 minutes. Turn over and cook for 2 minutes.

Divide the cooked pasta among your plates and top with equal amounts of sauce and scallops. Garnish with a pinch of pepper flakes and a sprinkle of parsley.

Ingredients

1 pound fettuccine
2 (5-ounce) packages Boursin cheese (any flavor)
2 cups heavy cream
Juice of 1/2 lemon
1 teaspoon salt
30 large sea scallops
1/4 cup extra-virgin olive oil
1 teaspoon salt
1 teaspoon black pepper
2 tablespoons extra-virgin olive oil
Crushed red pepper flakes
Chopped Italian parsley

MAKES SIX ENTRÉES OR TEN APPETIZERS

69

Spinach Lasagna

This is a nice change from the traditional meat lasagna we're all used to. It's good served just like this or topped with a marinara sauce.

Lasagna

3 tablespoons olive oil

3 red onions, sliced

1 1/2 pounds feta cheese, crumbled

2 pounds mozzarella cheese, shredded

1 recipe Béchamel

1 pound lasagna noodles, cooked

3 (10-ounce) boxes frozen chopped spinach, thawed and drained

Béchamel

1/4 cup (1/2 stick) butter

1 tablespoon diced onion

1/4 cup flour

5 cups milk

Salt to taste

White pepper to taste

Pinch of grated fresh nutmeg

Chef's Note

When making lasagna of any kind, I always use the "oven ready—no boil" pasta. One reason is obvious—it's faster and easier. The other reason is that no matter what I do when boiling lasagna noodles, they always end up torn and stuck together! Use whichever style you want. You'll probably need about 9 ounces of the "no boil" variety.

Lasagna

Heat the olive oil in a sauté pan. Add the red onions and cook until tender and caramelized, about 7 minutes. Set aside. Combine the cheeses. Set aside.

Spread some of the Béchamel in a large deep baking dish. Cover the sauce with a layer of the lasagna noodles. Spread 1/3 of the onions over the noodles, followed by 1/4 of the Béchamel, 1/3 of the spinach and 1/4 of the cheese mixture. Top with another layer of the noodles and press down. Repeat the layers, finishing with a layer of the noodles. Spread the remaining Béchamel over the top and finish with the last of the cheese. Bake in a 350-degree oven for 45 to 60 minutes. Let stand 15 minutes before serving.

Béchamel

Melt the butter in a saucepan. Add the onion and cook until translucent. Add the flour and cook over low heat for about 8 minutes, stirring frequently. Do not brown the onions or the flour.

Pour in the milk and whisk until well-incorporated. Simmer for 45 minutes or until thick. Season to taste with salt, white pepper and nutmeg.

Pasta alla Puttanesca

It is said that the prostitutes in Italy created the puttanesca. It's quick, easy to make, and could be prepared between customers! If you take a look at the recipe, you'll see that the entire thing can be made while the pasta is boiling. I first learned to make it while I was a student at the Culinary Institute of America. There, I was taught that the drained, hot noodles were enough to heat the ingredients that make up the sauce. Since then, others have told me that they cook everything in a little olive oil. I prefer the former method, especially when using fresh tomatoes, which I think are the best choice when making a puttanesca.

Prepare the pasta using the package directions. Set aside.

Place the tomatoes, capers, olives, red chile, olive oil and basil in a large mixing bowl.

Place the garlic and anchovies on a cutting board and sprinkle with the salt. Chop the garlic and anchovies coarsely. Crush the garlic and anchovies with the side of a knife blade, using the salt as an abrasive. Crush until puréed. Add the purée to the mixing bowl.

Add the pasta to the tomato mixture and toss gently. Serve immediately topped with cheese.

Ingredients

1 pound pasta, any variety

1 3/4 pounds fresh tomatoes, diced, or 1 (28-ounce) can chopped tomatoes, drained

1 tablespoon capers

1/2 cup sliced kalamata olives (or other olives)

1 teaspoon crushed red chile (optional)

Splash of extra-virgin olive oil

1 (2/3-ounce) bunch fresh basil, julienned

2 garlic cloves

3 anchovies

1 teaspoon kosher salt

Grated Parmesan cheese

Rigatoni with Tuna Sauce

One morning at 2:15, as a friend of mine was packing for a week's vacation in the Sonoma Valley of the California Wine Country, we wrote this recipe over the phone. Her flight was at 7:00 a.m., and I'm glad she spent a few minutes helping me with this recipe because when I tested it the next day, I decided that it was one of the best pasta dishes I had ever had. It only works, though, when using imported tuna in olive oil—preferably in big pieces. Once you try it, you'll understand why I make it over and over again.

Ingredients

10 1/2 ounces tuna in olive oil

5 garlic cloves, minced

1 (28-ounce) can diced tomatoes, with juice

1 teaspoon salt

1/2 teaspoon freshly ground black pepper

1 tablespoon crushed red pepper flakes

1/4 cup chopped Italian parsley

1 pound rigatoni, cooked

Grated Parmigiano-Reggiano cheese

Heat the oil from the tuna in a large sauté pan over medium-high heat. Add the garlic and sauté for a minute. Add the tomatoes with juice, salt, pepper and pepper flakes. Continue cooking for about 7 minutes, until the liquid has been reduced and the sauce becomes thicker.

At the last minute, add the tuna and the parsley. Mix carefully as you don't want to break up the tuna too much. Cook until the sauce gets hot again. Taste and adjust seasonings if necessary. Serve over the cooked rigatoni and top with grated cheese.

Perciatelli all'Amatriciana

Joe Saglimbeni, the owner of a fabulous wine, spirits, and gourmet
store in San Antonio, Texas, shared this recipe with me, telling me that it
was his favorite. It uses pancetta, an Italian-style bacon, for the main
flavoring. Joe explained to me that you really need to let this dish simmer
for a while so that the sauce has time to thicken. Although he makes
it with perciatelli, any long pasta will do.

In a large pan over a medium-high flame, heat the oil. Add the garlic, onion and pepper flakes and sauté for about 2 minutes. Add the pancetta, turn down the heat to medium, and continue cooking until the pancetta is done.

Once the pancetta is cooked, stir in the tomatoes and tomato paste along with the salt and pepper. Reduce the heat to low and simmer for 30 minutes. Add the basil, turn off the heat and let sit for 10 minutes before stirring into the cooked, hot perciatelli. Serve topped with grated cheese.

SERVES FOUR TO SIX

Ingredients

2 tablespoons olive oil
6 garlic cloves, minced
1/2 yellow onion
1 tablespoon crushed red pepper
    flakes
1/2 pound pancetta, diced
42 ounces chopped tomatoes
6 ounces tomato paste
1 teaspoon salt
1 teaspoon freshly ground
    black pepper
10 basil leaves, julienned
1 pound perciatelli, cooked
Grated Parmigiano-Reggiano to
    taste

Bucatini with Pepperoni-Meat Sauce

My Aunt Mague Flores-Nutt used to make a sauce almost exactly like this one. As I mentioned in the beginning of this chapter, I could live on pasta with red sauce, and this one with meat is no exception. The pepperoni gives it a unique flavor. One Sunday when the family was gathered around her table enjoying her spaghetti, I made the mistake of listening to my father and commenting to his sister, "Great Ragú!" After the entire room went silent, and I saw the look on her face, I knew then that I would never get to enjoy her homemade sauce again. Fortunately, after what seemed like an eternity, she laughed, and I spent many more Sundays seated at Aunt Mague's table, devouring her spaghetti.

Pepperoni-Meat Sauce

1 1/2 pounds ground beef
1 1/2 pounds sliced pepperoni
1 large yellow onion, diced
1 medium green bell pepper, diced
2 tablespoons Italian Seasonings
1/4 teaspoon cumin
1 tablespoon crushed red pepper flakes
2 (8-ounce) cans tomato sauce
2 (6-ounce) cans tomato paste
1 (10 3/4-ounce) can tomato purée
Salt to taste
1/2 cup red wine
2 pounds bucatini pasta, cooked

Italian Seasonings

2 tablespoons dried parsley
1 tablespoon dried thyme
2 tablespoon dried basil
1 1/2 tablespoons dried oregano
2 tablespoons garlic powder
2 ground bay leaves
1 teaspoon ground fennel seeds
1 teaspoon salt

Pepperoni-Meat Sauce

In a deep sauce pot, cook the ground beef, pepperoni, onion, bell pepper, Italian Seasonings, cumin and pepper flakes until browned and the fat is fried out of the pepperoni. If there is too much grease in the pan, drain before continuing.

Add the tomato sauce, paste and purée. Also add 1 can of water for every can of tomato product put in. Stir well and add salt if needed. Bring to a boil, turn heat down and simmer for 2 hours. Taste and adjust salt and Italian Seasonings if necessary. Add the wine and simmer for another 2 hours before serving over the cooked bucatini.

Italian Seasonings

Combine the parsley, thyme, basil and oregano. Add the garlic powder, bay leaves, fennel seeds and salt and mix together. Store in an airtight container in the refrigerator. Use as needed.

Apple-Cambozola Risotto

The key to good risotto is planning, patience, and plenty of hot stock. Other than that, it really is easy to make and can be flavored with a number of ingredients. Cheese is usually one of them. As you have seen, I use Cambozola in this particular risotto. Cambozola is basically a blue Brie.

SERVES FOUR TO SIX

Place the butter in a heavy-bottomed pot and start melting it over low heat. Meanwhile, core the apples and dice them. Set aside. Wash the green onions, cut off the roots, and slice thin up to the green stems.

Once the butter has melted, turn up the heat to medium-high and add the apples and green onions. Sauté for 3 minutes, stirring occasionally. Next add the Arborio rice and continue to cook and stir for 2 more minutes.

Turn heat down to medium and add 2 cups of the vegetable stock. Simmer for 5 minutes, stirring occasionally and scraping the bottom and edges of the pan.

After the 5 minutes, add 2 more cups of stock and continue to cook, stir, and scrape occasionally, for 10 more minutes.

After these 10 minutes have passed, add 2 more cups of the stock. Again, continue to simmer and stir for another 10 minutes.

Finally, add 1 more cup of stock, the salt and spices. Cook and stir for 5 minutes. When the 5 minutes is up, remove from the heat and add the brandy and cheese. Stir until the cheese is melted and well-combined. Serve immediately.

Ingredients

4 tablespoons (1/2 stick) butter
2 Granny Smith apples
1 bunch green onions
12 ounces Arborio rice
7 cups vegetable stock
2 teaspoons salt
Pinch of cinnamon
Pinch of cloves
Pinch of mace
Pinch of allspice
2 tablespoons applejack brandy
1/2 pound Cambozola cheese

Salmon with Spinach Fettuccine in an Alfredo Sauce

SERVES TWO

Once you have all of your ingredients gathered, the final dish takes no time to prepare. For an extra-special meal, reduce the amount of salmon and toss in your favorite shellfish, such as shrimp, mussels, or scallops.

Ingredients

1/2 cup (1 stick) butter
12 ounces fresh salmon fillet,
   cut into pieces
Salt
Coarsely ground black pepper
1 teaspoon minced garlic
1 pint heavy cream
1/4 cup grated Parmesan cheese
1/2 lemon
10 ounces fresh spinach
   fettuccine, cooked and cooled
2 tablespoons minced Italian
   parsley

Place a small pot of water on to boil. Melt the butter in a sauté pan over medium-high heat. Season the salmon with salt and pepper and place in the pan to cook. Cook for about 3 minutes and then add the garlic. Continuing cooking for another minute. Pour in the heavy cream and cook until it has reduced and thickened, about 5 minutes. Add the cheese. Squeeze in the lemon juice.

Drop the pasta into the boiling water and heat it for about 1 to 2 minutes. Drain it and add it to the pan. Toss well. Season with salt and pepper. Add the parsley. Divide among 2 plates and serve immediately.

Pestos

The following are several pesto recipes that I had originally created as part of my product line. Though my test market had nothing but high praises for them, in the end I decided not to produce them commercially. I now share them with you. The addition of vinegar and bread crumbs makes these pestos a little different from more traditional recipes. Initially, I did this to help make them shelf-stable (vinegar) and to stretch them out (bread crumbs). Normally I would not add those two ingredients to a pesto, but, since everyone liked them, I left them in. Enjoy these pestos not only atop pasta but also with any meat, seafood, vegetable, or poultry. Stir them into scrambled eggs or use them to make bruschetta.

Artichoke-Garlic-Basil Pesto

Place the artichokes, garlic, basil, almonds, balsamic vinegar and Parmesan cheese in a food processor and purée. With the motor running, pour in the olive oil until combined. Taste and add salt if you think it needs it.

Mushroom-Rosemary Pesto

Remove the leaves from the rosemary and discard the stems. Place in a food processor with the mushrooms, garlic, walnuts, cheese, balsamic vinegar, bread crumbs and lime juice and purée. With the motor running, pour in the olive oil until combined. Taste and add salt if you think it needs it.

Olive-Green Pepper Pesto

Place the olives, garlic, cheese, bell peppers, basil, almonds, balsamic vinegar and bread crumbs in a food processor and purée. With the motor running, pour in the olive oil until combined. Taste and add salt if you think it needs it.

MAKES THREE TO FOUR CUPS EACH

Artichoke-Garlic-Basil Pesto

2 (14-ounce) cans marinated
   artichokes
8 garlic cloves
3 ounces fresh basil
5 ounces almonds
3 tablespoons balsamic vinegar
1 cup grated Parmesan cheese
1 cup olive oil
Salt

Mushroom-Rosemary Pesto

2/3 ounce fresh rosemary
1 1/2 pounds fresh button
   mushrooms
4 garlic cloves
4 ounces walnuts
1 cup grated Parmesan cheese
1/3 cup balsamic vinegar
1/2 cup bread crumbs
Juice of 1/2 lime
1 1/2 cups olive oil

Olive-Green Pepper Pesto

10 ounces pimento-stuffed green
   olives
12 ounces black olives
5 garlic cloves
1 cup grated Parmesan cheese
3/4 pound green bell peppers
1 (2/3-ounce) bunch fresh basil
4 ounces almonds
1/4 cup balsamic vinegar
1/3 cup bread crumbs
3/4 cup olive oil

Old-Fashioned Italian Meatballs

MAKES ABOUT FORTY
MEATBALLS

I, or should I say we, are lucky that I was able to talk my friend Sue Leone into sharing this recipe. It is one of a handful in this book that remains exactly as it was given to me. Sue made me promise not to change a thing—I've tasted them before and knew that it would be an easy promise to keep. These meatballs are so good that my little brother Tommy, who has Down Syndrome, proposed to Sue after he tasted them! She explained that he would have to wine and dine her. He innocently asked why since she was a good cook! That sums it up: Sue Leone is a good cook, and these meatballs are proof. This is a recipe where I will instruct you not to change a thing, especially the number of eggs or the use of lard. If you feel you must, I would suggest not making them. It makes that big a difference.

Ingredients

2 pounds ground chuck or
  ground round
1 pound ground pork
18 eggs
2 cups plain bread crumbs
1 cup grated Parmigiano-
  Reggiano cheese
1 head garlic, minced
1/2 cup chopped fresh parsley
2 tablespoons salt
2 tablespoons freshly ground
  black pepper
1 pound lard for frying

Mix the ground beef and pork, eggs, bread crumbs, cheese, garlic, parsley, salt and pepper in a large bowl. (The best way to mix is with a gloved hand. The mixture is very sticky and needs to be mixed well.) Cover and refrigerate for at least 1 hour for easier handling. Heat the lard in a large deep skillet. Hand roll meatballs about the size of a golf ball (or smaller for soups or as an appetizer) and place them carefully in the hot grease (the grease will foam). When the pan is full, you may want to turn the heat down a bit. Let the meatballs fry until the redness is gone from the bottom and the meatballs are loose in the pan. Turn the meatballs over and finish cooking. Drain the meatballs on paper towels. (Save the grease in the refrigerator: it's great for fried potatoes.) These meatballs are delicious fresh fried or cooked in sauce for at least an hour.

Sue Leone notes: "I was always disappointed that my meatballs never seemed to be the right taste or consistency. Then my uncle Ange told me the secret: 'lots of eggs!!!' Not I nor anyone I have made them for has been disappointed since I started adding lots of eggs."

Rigatoni Toss

Here's another recipe that Sue Leone shared with me. She says that this is a lighter version of lasagna and is simply delicious!!! It immediately reminded me of a dish made by my cousin Rich Pennock's wife Carmela's mother, and that I enjoyed while living in New York.

SERVES FOUR TO SIX

Sauce

In a large saucepan, sauté about 8 large cloves of chopped garlic in olive oil. Add the tomatoes, tomato paste, water, salt, black and red pepper and parsley.

Cook, covered, over medium heat for 2 to 3 hours. You should have plenty of sauce for a second meal.

Meat

While your sauce is cooking, sauté the garlic, ground pork and ground veal in the olive oil in a skillet. Break meat apart while cooking.

Assembly

When your sauce is ready, toss 1 pound cooked rigatoni with just enough sauce to coat. Add the meat and the ricotta cheese and toss gently.

Top with more sauce. Garnish with Parmigiano-Reggiano cheese and Italian parsley.

Sauce

8 garlic cloves, chopped
Olive oil
2 (28-ounce) cans diced tomatoes
1 (36-ounce) can whole peeled tomatoes in juice, puréed
1 (12-ounce) can tomato paste
25 ounces water
1 tablespoon salt
1 teaspoon freshly ground black pepper
1 tablespoon crushed red pepper
1 tablespoon chopped fresh Italian parsley

Meat

3 garlic cloves, chopped
1 pound ground pork
1 pound ground veal
2 tablespoons olive oil

Assembly

1 pound rigatoni, cooked
1 pound ricotta cheese
Grated Parmigiano-Reggiano cheese
Chopped fresh Italian parsley

Garlic-Vegetable Penne

This pasta takes no time to make and has a brilliant result. If you're watching calories, try substituting light or nonfat sour cream for the heavy cream. This also makes a great meal during Lent if you replace the chicken broth with clam juice or fish stock.

Ingredients

1 pound penne pasta, cooked
  al dente and drained
6 to 8 garlic cloves, sliced
Olive oil
1 cup sliced fresh carrots
1 bunch broccoli florets, trimmed
1 cup chicken broth
1 small package frozen sweet
  peas, thawed
1/2 cup heavy cream
1 teaspoon each salt and pepper
2 tablespoons chopped Italian
  parsley
Grated Parmigiano-Reggiano
  cheese

In a large sauté pan, sauté the garlic in olive oil until slightly brown but not burned. Add the carrots, broccoli and chicken broth. Cook until the vegetables are soft. Add the peas, cream, salt and pepper. Turn the heat to low and toss in the penne. Cook for 2 to 3 minutes. Let stand for 5 minutes before serving. Taste and adjust seasonings if necessary. Garnish with parsley and cheese.

Spaghetti with Sausage and Mushrooms

Enjoy this pasta on a brisk fall night with a glass of bold red wine. It's important to use a good Italian sausage for this dish.

Ingredients

5 to 6 garlic cloves, sliced
2 tablespoons chopped onion
1 large fresh carrot, sliced
3 tablespoons olive oil
1 pound Italian sausage
1/4 cup red wine
1/2 pound fresh mushrooms, sliced
1 (28-ounce) can diced tomatoes
  in juice
2 tablespoons Italian Seasonings
  (page 74)
1 tablespoon crushed red pepper
1 teaspoon each salt and pepper
1 pound spaghetti
Grated Parmigiano-Reggiano
  cheese

In large saucepan, sauté the garlic, onion and carrots in the olive oil. Cut the sausage into 1/2-inch slices. Add the sausage and wine to the saucepan and cook until all of the pink is gone from the sausage. Add the mushrooms, tomatoes with the juice and the Italian seasoning, red pepper, salt and black pepper. Cook on low for about 45 minutes. Cook the spaghetti using the package directions and drain well. Serve the sauce over the freshly cooked spaghetti with the cheese.

Spaghetti with Arugula

Here's another one of those quick toss pastas that's easy to prepare in a hurry. Your outcome will be successful as long as you use fresh ingredients and good Parmigiano-Reggiano.

Cook the spaghetti according to the directions on the package. While the pasta is cooking, heat the olive oil and sauté the garlic and chile peppers.

During the last 2 minutes of the pasta cooking, add the arugula to the pot of boiling spaghetti. Drain well and place in a serving bowl. Stir in the garlic, chiles and hot oil. Season to taste. Garnish with cheese. Serve at once.

SERVES FOUR TO SIX

Ingredients
1 pound spaghetti
4 tablespoons olive oil
5 garlic cloves, minced
1 or 2 small chile peppers (such as serrano or Thai), thinly sliced
5 ounces arugula leaves
Grated Parmigiano-Reggiano cheese
Juice of 1/2 lemon

Ditalini and Beans

It's been only recently that I eat beans with my pasta. At first, I thought it to be such a strange concept—until I tried it. You too need to try it, if you never have. This recipe is pretty quick and quite good.

In a large sauce pot over medium-low heat, sauté the bacon and garlic until golden. Add the beans in liquid and cook on medium-low for about 10 minutes. Add the tomatoes in juice, tomato paste, water, black pepper, salt, red pepper and parsley. Bring to a boil. Reduce the heat and simmer for about 40 minutes, stirring occasionally to prevent burning.

Cook the pasta. When al dente, stir the pasta into the sauce with 1 cup of pasta cooking water. Cook on low for about 10 minutes. Let stand for about 10 minutes before serving. Serve with grated cheese and crusty Italian bread.

SERVES FOUR TO SIX

Ingredients
1/2 pound bacon or pancetta, chopped
5 to 6 garlic cloves, thinly sliced
1 (19-ounce) can cannellini or great Northern beans
1 large can tomatoes in juice, puréed in blender
1 (6-ounce) can tomato paste
1 (6-ounce) tomato paste can water
1/2 teaspoon black pepper
2 teaspoons salt
1 tablespoon crushed red pepper
1 tablespoon chopped fresh Italian parsley
1 pound ditalini pasta
1 cup water, reserved from cooking pasta
Grated Parmigiano-Reggiano cheese

ON
THE
SIDE

*V*egetables and starches are an important part of an entrée, or main course. Actually, they are an essential part of any meal and of our diet. Not only do they contribute to our daily food requirements (you know, the pyramid and all that stuff), but they help in the presentation of entrées! The plate looks so much nicer when the veal chop is leaned up against golden mashed potatoes, or a succulent fillet of red snapper is presented atop perfectly cooked rice pilaf.

I don't have much to say about vegetables except that, in general, we rarely eat enough, and I'm not sure why. I think it's because, unlike in most of the world, the vegetables in this country are available all of the time, whether at peak season or not. Consequently, the vegetables we eat are not always at their best in terms of flavor. I might even say they are sometimes bland or even tasteless. However, I have an easy remedy for this. First of all, you could grow your own vegetables. The flavors are so incredibly different that once you do this, you will never buy produce from a grocery store again. Growing and harvesting vegetables, I know, is far easier said than done. The next best thing is to buy a book or do some research on the Internet to learn the exact seasons of fruits and vegetables. Trust me, whether you undertake gardening or spend time doing the research, it will lead to a greater appreciation of vegetables and a much healthier life.

When it comes to starches, there are no restrictions on how they should be served or what they should accompany. I, however, have my own thoughts on this matter. In my opinion, potatoes of any kind should accompany only beef, fowl, or pork. Never serve potatoes with fish (the fried seafood platter with French fries and hush puppies is an exception). Since fish is more delicate than meat, I think it's best served with any kind of rice, grain, or pasta. Remember, this is my opinion. You present your meal as you wish it to be served. Again, there are no strict rules as to what should be served with what. If there were, and you followed them too closely, cooking would become tedious, a chore almost, and no fun. Cooking should be a source of enjoyment.

You will find in this SIDE DISHES section that I have included more starches than vegetables. That's because I think cooking vegetables is a "no-brainer." As long as you start with delicious, fresh-tasting veggies, you can't go wrong. If nothing else, blanch and shock vegetables with a cold water bath; then reheat and toss them in butter with minced shallots, salt, and freshly ground black pepper. Alternatively, steam or roast vegetables and season them to taste—Mother Nature takes care of the rest.

What I have included in this section are fantastic-tasting starches. If you are a true Irishman like my pastor, Father Patrick O'Shea, you'll especially enjoy this section. I think he has a spud at every meal. When I mentioned I was tired of eating them, he threatened to take me before the Archbishop! Mind you, my comment was made the day after we tested every potato recipe in the book.

On the Side

Asparagus in Mignonette Sauce

In the directions below, I tell you to serve the Mignonette Sauce warm over the asparagus. As another option, serve the entire dish chilled. That's how I usually eat them—and with my fingers, of course. The sauce really should be loaded down with shallots and should only be made with freshly ground pepper—out of a tin won't do. This sauce is also great spooned over oysters on the half shell, as I first had it. One last idea: for a nice salad, serve the entire dish cold, over a bed of mixed greens.

In a bowl, combine the lemon juice, shallots, 1 teaspoon kosher salt, pepper and olive oil. Set aside.

Cut the bottoms off of the asparagus (about 3 inches) and discard. (Or save them for a vegetable stock!)

Fill a large pot with water and 1/4 cup salt. Bring to a boil. Once a rolling boil has been achieved, drop in the asparagus and blanch for 1 minute and 30 seconds. Remove from the heat and serve IMMEDIATELY topped with the sauce or drop immediately into ice cold water to stop the cooking.

If doing the latter, drain on paper towels. When ready to serve, top with the sauce that has been heated in the microwave for about 1 minute or just until warm to the touch.

Ingredients
1/2 cup fresh lemon juice
1/4 cup minced shallots
1 teaspoon kosher salt
2 tablespoons coarsely ground black pepper
1/4 cup extra-virgin olive oil
1 bunch fresh asparagus
1/4 cup kosher salt

Candied Brussels Sprouts with Chestnuts

Even those weary of Brussels sprouts will enjoy this recipe. It's great served at fall or winter holiday feasts. I suggest finding canned or jarred chestnuts at a gourmet specialty store—they usually have them, and it will make your life a lot easier.

Cut an "X" in the bottom of each of the Brussels sprouts, no deeper than 1/4 inch. Drop into a pot of rapidly boiling water for a long count of 10. Remove to a large bowl full of ice and water to stop the cooking. Remove from the ice water and set aside.

Melt the butter in a large pan over high heat. Add the chestnuts, brown sugar, nutmeg, cardamom and salt and cook on high until the brown sugar is well-dissolved. Turn the heat to medium and continue cooking until thick and syrupy, about 20 minutes. Adjust the seasonings.

Ingredients
2 pounds fresh Brussels sprouts
8 tablespoons (1 stick) butter
1 pound chestnuts, roasted and shelled
1 1/2 cups packed brown sugar
1/2 teaspoon grated fresh nutmeg
1/2 teaspoon cardamom
1 teaspoon salt

Herb Roasted Beets in Balsamic Vinegar

I only recently discovered that beets are such a great vegetable. Once when I was dining in New York City, some were served to me tossed in a vinaigrette, and I fell in love with them immediately. They are so versatile and can take on any flavor you decide to give them. Beets are good served hot or cold. I've gotten used to eating them in the manner served to me in New York City. That is, boiled, peeled, and chilled, with a light Champagne vinaigrette. (They also work wonders when added to a pot of pears being poached in red wine—you can't beat the color they impart.) This recipe comes from a series of cooking classes I was asked to teach for a fund-raiser at Saint Anthony de Padua Catholic Church in San Antonio, Texas.

SERVES FIVE TO SEVEN

Ingredients

- 1/3 cup balsamic vinegar
- 1/3 cup honey
- 1/2 cup (1 stick) butter
- 1/2 cup extra-virgin olive oil
- 4 to 6 beets, stems removed
- 1 teaspoon kosher salt
- 1 teaspoon coarsely ground black pepper
- Herbs and spices of your choice

Preheat the oven to 400 degrees.

In the microwave or on top of the stove, combine the balsamic vinegar, honey, butter and olive oil. Heat until the butter is melted.

Place the cleaned beets in an oven baking bag (it makes cleanup easier) and pour the balsamic vinegar mixture in, along with the salt, pepper and herbs and seasonings of your choice. Close the bag, place in a 13×9-inch baking pan and bake for 1 hour. Turn off the oven and let sit for another 30 minutes.

Alternatively, line a 13×9-inch pan with foil. Add the cleaned beets to the pan and pour the balsamic mixture over them. Season with the salt, pepper and herbs and seasonings of your choice. Close the foil over the beets and roast for 1 hour at 400 degrees. Turn off the oven and allow to rest for 30 minutes. To serve, cut the tops and bottoms off of the beets. Using your fingers or a paring knife, remove the skins. Next, cut the beets in half (north to south). Finally, cut the beets into wedges and serve with the cooking liquid spooned over them.

Tarragon-White Grape Carrots

This recipe is so easy it's ridiculous! And it's foolproof to boot. These carrots have always met with applause when I've served them, both at home and in restaurants. It's a great vegetable to take to a party. Just reheat them when you get there. You can even double the amount of carrots without adding more grape juice. The other nice thing about this dish is that neither salt nor pepper is required.

Combine the carrots, tarragon and grape juice concentrate in a sauce pan and simmer over low heat, uncovered, for about 45 minutes to an hour—or to the desired doneness.

Ingredients
1 pound carrots, matchstick cut
1 tablespoon dry tarragon
1 (11½-ounce) can frozen white grape juice concentrate, thawed

Carrot-Maple Pudding

There is no problem multiplying this recipe for larger crowds. And before you ask, yes, it really does need the heavy cream. It contributes to the pudding's overall texture and richness. Once you try it, you'll understand what I mean. The only other thing I can say about this recipe is: "Delicious!"

Toss the carrots with the oil, put on a baking sheet and roast for 1 hour and 30 minutes at 375 degrees. When the carrots are done, put them in a food processor or blender along with the maple syrup, eggs, egg yolks, nutmeg, cloves, allspice, mace and cinnamon. Add the cream and pecans. Pulse just until blended. (Do not overprocess or the cream will break.) Pour the carrot mixture into a buttered 9×9-inch pan and top with pieces of the butter. Bake in a 350-degree oven for 30 minutes. Allow to rest for about 10 minutes before scooping out and serving.

Ingredients
2 pounds carrots, peeled and sliced into 1- to 2-inch pieces
3 tablespoons vegetable oil
½ cup maple syrup
3 eggs
2 egg yolks
Dash of nutmeg
¼ teaspoon ground cloves
¼ teaspoon ground allspice
Dash of mace
½ teaspoon cinnamon
1½ cup heavy cream
½ cup pecans
2 tablespoons butter, cut into pieces

Curry Roasted Cauliflower

SERVES SIX TO EIGHT

Ingredients

1 large head cauliflower
1/2 cup fresh lemon juice
1 teaspoon kosher salt
1 tablespoon curry powder
2 tablespoons extra-virgin
   olive oil
1 teaspoon chile powder
1 cup plain yogurt

If you are not a fan of curry, steer clear of this recipe. If you do like curry, then this one's for you. The whole head of cauliflower makes a gorgeous presentation at your table. To serve, pass it around and let people dig in. It breaks apart relatively easily after it's been roasted.

Preheat the oven to 350 degrees. Place the cauliflower head in a deep ovenproof pot with a lid or a 9×9-inch glass baking dish. Pour the lemon juice in the bottom of the pot or baking dish. In a small bowl, combine the salt, curry powder, oil and chile powder. Rub the mixture over the cauliflower. Place a lid on the pot or cover with foil and roast for 50 minutes. When the time is up, pour the yogurt over the cauliflower and continue roasting, uncovered, for 15 more minutes. Serve the cauliflower in a deep bowl or platter with the cooking juices from the pot or baking dish poured over the top.

Italian Greens & Beans

SERVES EIGHT

Ingredients

1 bunch broccoli raab
1 bunch mustard greens
5 to 6 garlic cloves, minced
3 tablespoons olive oil
1 can cannellini or great
   Northern beans
1 cup chicken broth
2 teaspoons crushed red pepper
1 teaspoon salt
1/2 teaspoon freshly ground
   black pepper

I went back and forth as to what section this dish should be under. It started with the soups, but I decided it was not soupy enough (a little more broth would do the trick if you are interested, though). Next, it moved to the appetizers and was being served with crusty bread. Finally, it ended up here under side dishes, with the only real reason being that I wanted more vegetables in this section! It's a delicious way to get your greens and fiber. If you can't find the two different types of leaves, just double up on one.

Snip off the ends of the broccoli raab and mustard greens, wash, cut into 2- to 3-inch lengths and drain well.

In deep sauce pan over medium-high heat, sauté the garlic in the olive oil until golden, about 2 minutes. Add the beans and liquid, chicken broth, red pepper, salt and black pepper. Bring to a simmer. Add the greens and stir until well-combined and the leaves start wilting. Cover, turn the heat to low, and cook until the greens are tender.

Eggplant in Romesco Sauce with Manchego Cheese

In 1996, at the 11th annual Texas Hill Country Wine and Food Festival, this was one of the dishes that helped me win the coveted "People's Choice Award." It not only makes a good side dish but is also able to stand on its own. The Romesco Sauce is scrumptious with grilled tuna or shrimp as well.

Eggplant

Peel the eggplants, quarter lengthwise and slice thinly. Place in a colander and sprinkle with salt. Set in a sink for a couple of hours. Rinse well and pat dry with paper towels. Heat half of the olive oil in a large sauté pan and add half of the eggplant. Cook until golden brown and remove from pan to drain on paper towels. Repeat the process with the remaining olive oil and eggplant. Allow the eggplant to completely cool and then place it in a large bowl.

Mix in the Manchego cheese, green onions, red bell pepper, green olives and Romesco Sauce. Refrigerate for several hours to overnight. Serve at room temperature.

Romesco Sauce

Roast the tomato and garlic in an ungreased roasting pan at 350 degrees for 30 minutes. Place the dried red pepper in a sauce pan with the water and 3 tablespoons of the vinegar. Bring to a boil, cover and simmer for 5 minutes.

Cut a 1/4-inch-thick slice lengthwise from the center of the baguette. Reserve the remaining bread for another purpose. Heat some of the olive oil and fry the bread in the oil until golden brown on both sides (you may have to add more oil). Transfer the bread to a food processor or blender. In the same oil, fry the almonds until golden brown (you may have to add more oil). Add the almonds to the food processor along with the boiled red pepper, pepper flakes, garlic and tomato. With the motor running, gradually pour in the remaining olive oil and vinegar. Add the lemon juice, salt and pepper. Purée until smooth. Taste! Adjust the seasonings with the salt and pepper. Store in the refrigerator. Serve at room temperature.

Eggplant

2 eggplants
Kosher salt
1/2 cup olive oil
2 cups grated Manchego cheese
2 green onions, thinly sliced
1 red bell pepper, roasted and diced
1 cup sliced green olives
1 cup Romesco Sauce

Romesco Sauce

1 large tomato
5 garlic cloves, peeled
1 dried sweet red pepper (New Mexico style)
1/2 cup water
11 tablespoons sherry vinegar
1 baguette
1 1/2 cups olive oil
12 blanched almonds
1/2 teaspoon crushed red pepper flakes
Juice of 1 lemon
1 teaspoon salt
1/2 teaspoon freshly ground black pepper

Eggplant Provençal

If you like eggplant the way I do, then you will really enjoy this recipe. The herbs used are the fresh version of dried French fines herbes and contribute greatly to the overall flavor of this vegetable dish. You can eat this alone or alongside some nice sautéed fish.

Ingredients

2 eggplants, halved lengthwise
Salt and freshly ground
    black pepper
1/4 cup olive oil
4 tomatoes, chopped
1 yellow onion, chopped
1 shallot, minced
5 garlic cloves, minced
1 tablespoon capers
1/4 cup red wine
2 tablespoons fresh basil
2 tablespoons chopped chives
2 tablespoons chervil
2 tablespoons parsley
2 tablespoons tarragon
1 teaspoon salt
1 teaspoon freshly ground
    black pepper
1 cup feta cheese
1 lemon, thinly sliced

Make a few slits in the skin of the eggplants with a knife. Season with some salt and pepper. Heat the olive oil in a sauté pan over medium-high heat and cook the eggplants cut side down for about 10 minutes. Turn the eggplants over and cook for an additional 10 minutes. You may need to continue to add oil as you sauté the eggplants. Drain on paper towels.

Next, sauté the tomatoes, onion, shallot and garlic in the oil. Add the capers, red wine, herbs and 1 teaspoon each salt and pepper.

Arrange the eggplant halves in a baking dish and cover with the tomato and herb mixture. Sprinkle with feta cheese and bake in a 425-degree oven for 25 minutes. Garnish with thin slices of lemon before serving.

Country-Style Mashed Potatoes with Goat Cheese & Roasted Garlic

I refer to these as country-style because the potatoes are not peeled before mashing. I think the peel adds a nice texture when broken up, not to mention some extra nutrients.

Roasted Garlic

Cut the top off of the head of garlic, top with the butter and wrap in foil.

Potatoes

Toss the unpeeled potatoes in the olive oil with the salt and pepper. Place in a roasting pan along with the foil-wrapped garlic and roast in a 350-degree oven for 1 hour and 30 minutes.

Assembly

Using an electric beater, whip the potatoes (skin on) with the goat cheese, butter and cream. Squeeze all of the garlic out of the skins and add to the potatoes. Whip again to combine but do not overmix. Taste and adjust the seasonings before serving.

Roasted Garlic

1 head of garlic
2 tablespoons butter

Potatoes

2 pounds small red or new
   potatoes
3 tablespoons olive oil
1 teaspoon salt
1 teaspoon freshly ground
   black pepper

Assembly

5 ounces goat cheese, at room
   temperature
4 tablespoons (1/2 stick) butter,
   softened
1/2 cup heavy cream, at room
   temperature or hot

Rosa's Chile Cheese Potatoes

SERVES SIX TO EIGHT

Growing up, these potatoes were somewhat of a staple in my house. They were prepared by our longtime housekeeper, Rosa Alaniz. Rosa came to work for my family (purely out of accident) in 1975. She helped my mother with the cooking and taught me some of my kitchen skills. My brother Tommy especially loved these potatoes. Actually, he likes potatoes of any kind, and Rosa was always making them for him. When creating the outline for this chapter, I knew I had to share this recipe with you. I got in the kitchen with Rosa, who not only still works for us but is also now part of the family, and followed her, writing down exact measurements and times. These make a great addition to her enchiladas, which you will find in the Tex and Mex section of this book. Often, though, we enjoyed them just by themselves.

Ingredients

5 small to medium tomatoes
2 fresh jalapeño chiles
2 teaspoons salt
2 tablespoons (about) water
4 potatoes, peeled
2 tablespoons corn oil
1/2 large white onion, sliced
2 garlic cloves, sliced
2 teaspoons salt
1 1/2 cups (about) water
2 cups shredded mozzarella
   cheese

Start off by placing the tomatoes and jalapeños on a hot griddle and charring on all sides. (This will probably take about 30 minutes and lots of patience.) The tops and bottoms are easy; the sides are a little more difficult. Consider the tomato a box with four sides. After the tops and bottoms are done, they will be soft enough to force the tomatoes on their sides.

When done, remove each tomato and jalapeño chile to a damp paper towel and wrap until cool enough to handle. Once cool enough, remove the skins and discard; this does not have to be totally perfect.

Place the jalapeños in a blender with 2 teaspoons of salt and about 2 tablespoons of water and purée. Next add the tomatoes and pulse just until blended. (You do not want a smooth purée.) Set aside.

Cut the potatoes in half from top to bottom, and then in half again from top to bottom. Slice the potatoes into thin pieces, about 1/8 inch thick. Set aside.

In a large pan with a lid, heat the corn oil. Sauté the onion and garlic for about 7 minutes over medium-low heat.

Turn the heat to high and add the potatoes, 2 teaspoons salt and the reserved tomato sauce. Top off with about 1 1/2 cups water and carefully stir well. Bring to a boil. Reduce the heat to low, cover and simmer for about 40 minutes, or until the potatoes are just soft (not mushy). Remove from the heat. Taste and adjust the seasonings with salt if necessary. Add the cheese and carefully stir until melted.

Avocado-Potato Hash

To be honest, I ran across the words "avocado-potato hash"
in one of my notebooks and cannot, for the life of me, begin to tell you
where I got the idea. It stuck in my mind and eventually turned into the
following recipe. Everyone who was in the test kitchen on the day
I made it absolutely fell in love with it. I think you will, too.

Bake the potatoes for 1 hour in a 350-degree oven. Allow to cool until you can handle them. Once cool enough to handle, peel the potatoes, discarding the peels. Using a box grater or food processor equipped with a grater blade, grate the potatoes, onion and garlic. Place in a bowl. Dice the avocado and add to the bowl along with the salt, cumin, pepper, chile powder, and vinegar. Carefully combine.

In a large sauté pan, heat the corn oil over a medium-high flame. Add the potato mixture and pat down evenly over the entire pan. Cook for 15 minutes. After 15 minutes, mix well, pat down and sauté for 5 more minutes. When 5 minutes are up, mix again. Repeat this process 2 more times. After this time has elapsed, taste and adjust the seasonings with salt if needed. Serve immediately. The hash should be crusty.

SERVES SIX TO EIGHT

Ingredients

2 pounds potatoes
1/2 yellow onion
5 garlic cloves
4 avocados
2 teaspoons kosher salt
1/2 teaspoon cumin
2 teaspoons freshly ground
     black pepper
1 teaspoon chile powder
2 tablespoons cider vinegar
3 tablespoons corn oil

Spaghetti Squash

Don't be afraid to tackle the spaghetti squash; just be careful.
It takes a good, long, sharp knife to hack into it. Once you do, you'll
enjoy this simple recipe that is sure to become a staple.

Preheat the oven to 375 degrees. Using a large kitchen knife, cut the squash in half from top to bottom. Remove the seeds and season the inside with salt and pepper. Put about 1 inch of water in a baking pan that is large enough to hold both sides of the squash cut side down. Roast for 1 hour and 15 minutes. When done, allow the squash halves to cool until you can handle them.

Using a fork, remove the squash from the tough skins (it should look like spaghetti) into a bowl. Add extra-virgin olive oil, cumin and basil. Slice the tomato into quarters and cut the seeds out. Dice the tomato and add to the squash mixture. Lightly toss, taste and adjust the seasonings with salt and pepper if needed. Serve warm.

SERVES FOUR

Ingredients

1 large spaghetti squash
Salt to taste
Freshly ground black pepper
     to taste
2 tablespoons extra-virgin
     olive oil
1 teaspoon ground cumin
Fresh basil (about 3 to 4 leaves),
     julienned
1 tomato

Mashed Chipotle Sweet Potatoes

SERVES SIX TO EIGHT

These mashed sweet potatoes offer a nice departure from the traditional ones we are all so familiar with. Canned chipotles in adobo sauce should be easy to find in the "ethnic" section of your local supermarket. Add more or fewer chiles depending on your palate. If you are really timid when it comes to chiles, try just adding some of the adobo sauce.

Ingredients

2 1/2 pounds sweet potatoes
1/4 cup maple syrup
2 chipotle peppers in adobo sauce, finely minced
8 tablespoons (1 stick) butter, softened
2 teaspoons salt
Juice of 1 lime
1/2 teaspoon vanilla extract

Peel the sweet potatoes and cube them. Place in a large pot with enough cold water to cover. Place over high heat and bring to a boil. Once boiling, continue cooking for 15 minutes or until tender. Drain and place in the bowl of an electric mixer with the maple syrup, chipotle peppers, butter, salt, lime juice and vanilla. Whip with the paddle attachment until smooth. (Or you can use an electric hand mixer or a handheld potato smasher.)

Sweet Potatoes with an Orange-Cumin Glaze

SERVES SIX TO EIGHT

This is another one of those no-brainer side dishes that's really easy to make, even for the most inexperienced of cooks. Though simple to prepare, the flavors are rich and deep. It even makes for a nice departure from the marshmallow-topped dish we often see at the Thanksgiving table.

Ingredients

2 to 2 1/2 pounds sweet potatoes, peeled
2 teaspoons salt
1 tablespoon ground cumin
1 (12-ounce) can pulp-free frozen orange juice concentrate, thawed

Cut the sweet potatoes into large chunks (they do not have to be perfect). Place in a glass or non-reactive baking pan and toss with the salt, cumin and orange juice. Roast in a 350-degree oven for 1 hour and 5 minutes.

Apples Stuffed with Mushrooms

These delicious stuffed apples were cooked up for a television appearance I made on the Patsy Swendson Show. *They are a great accompaniment for any roasted fowl.*

Cut off the top of the apples about 1/8 inch down. Set the tops aside. Hollow out the inside of each apple, leaving a thick but sturdy shell. Rub the inside of each apple with the lemon juice. Remove the seeds and chop the scooped-out apple pulp.

In a large pan, melt the butter. Add the garlic and shallot and sauté for about 1 minute. Add the chopped apples and sliced mushrooms. Continue to sauté until the mixture is cooked and begins to dry out. Add the Madeira. Stir in the crema Mexicana and herbs. Simmer until it begins to thicken. Season with the salt and pepper. Set aside.

Season the inside of the apples. Spoon the mushroom mixture into the apple cups, dividing evenly (it is okay for the filling to come over the top). Place the reserved tops on top of the stuffed apples. Place the apples in a greased baking dish small enough to hold them tightly. Pour the stock, wine and cider around the apples. Bake, uncovered, in a 350-degree oven for 45 minutes to an hour, depending on the size of the apples. If the apples begin to get too brown during baking, cover them with foil. Serve warm.

Ingredients

4 large baking apples
Juice of 1 lemon
4 tablespoons (1/2 stick) butter
3 garlic cloves, minced
1 shallot, chopped
3/4 pound assorted mushrooms, sliced
1 ounce Madeira
1/4 cup crema Mexicana or crème fraîche
1/4 cup chopped herbs
1 teaspoon salt
1 teaspoon freshly ground black pepper
3 tablespoons chicken stock
3 tablespoons white wine
3 tablespoons apple cider

Smoked Gouda Polenta

To me, polenta is one of those things that is either good or bad . . . nowhere in between. This one is good and is achieved by patience and diligent stirring. It may be served immediately in the style of mashed potatoes or poured into a baking pan and allowed to stiffen. When serving it in the latter fashion, cut it into diamonds and grill, quickly sauté, or bake to reheat. To serve, top with your favorite sauce or vegetable, if desired.

SERVES SIX TO EIGHT

Ingredients

1 shallot, chopped

2 garlic cloves, minced

1/2 teaspoon crushed red pepper flakes

2 tablespoons butter

2 cups chicken broth

2 cups heavy cream

1 1/4 cups yellow cornmeal

7 ounces smoked Gouda cheese, shredded

1 egg, beaten

Salt to taste

Freshly ground black pepper to taste

Sauté the shallots, garlic and pepper flakes in butter over medium-high heat for 3 minutes. Add the broth and cream and bring to a boil. Slowly whisk in the cornmeal. Simmer the mixture for 45 minutes over low heat, stirring often, making sure to scrape the bottom and corners of the pot.

Remove from the heat and stir in the cheese, followed by the egg, and combine well. Taste and season with salt and pepper. Serve immediately. To reheat, stir in more broth or cream in order to reach the desired consistency.

Irish Potato Stuffing

An old Catholic priest from Ireland shared this one with me. He said that it has been used in his family for generations to stuff turkeys. I have found that it also is delicious stuffed in chicken, duck, or Cornish hens. It's even great spread out on the bottom of a pan, topped with seasoned chicken pieces, and roasted in the oven.

MAKES FOUR TO FIVE CUPS

Ingredients

4 baking potatoes, peeled

1 white onion, chopped

3 to 4 garlic cloves, minced

2 teaspoons salt

2 teaspoons freshly ground black pepper

1 1/2 cups croutons

1 stick (8 tablespoons) butter, melted

6 to 10 basil leaves, thinly sliced

2 tablespoons water

Cut the potatoes into large cubes and boil until soft, about 15 to 20 minutes. Drain and allow to cool. Place the potatoes in a large bowl with the onion, garlic, salt and pepper. Add the croutons, butter, basil and water and mash with your (clean) hands. Taste and adjust seasonings if necessary. Stuff any bird you desire. (Place extra stuffing under and around the bird.) Roast the bird until done.

Calamari Jasmine Rice

For this recipe, you will want to use a long grain, jasmine-flavored rice.
I use Jasmati® brand, which combines traditional American
long grain rice with unique and exotic Asian jasmine rice. It is readily
available in the rice section of grocery and health food stores. The snowy
white rice, with its rich aroma, combines nicely with the delicate white
calamari for a stunning combination that pleases all of your senses. This
dish is good by itself, with fried fish, and even meat. Also, try it topped
with grilled or stir-fried vegetables.

Preheat the oven to 350 degrees. In a small ovenproof pot, heat the butter and oil over medium-high heat until hot and bubbly. Add the calamari, green onions, garlic, lemon grass and bay leaf. Cook, stirring frequently, for 5 minutes. Next add the rice, salt and pepper, and continue cooking for 2 more minutes, stirring constantly. Finally, stir in the hot water and scrape the bottom of the pot. Bring to a boil. Cover and place in the oven for 25 minutes. When done, remove the lemon grass and bay leaf before serving.

Ingredients

2 tablespoons butter
2 tablespoons extra-virgin
    olive oil
1/4 pound calamari, sliced into
    1/8-inch rings
2 green onions, sliced
1 garlic clove, minced
1 piece lemon grass
    (about 1/2 inch long), bruised
1 bay leaf
1 cup Jasmati® rice or any other
    jasmine-flavored rice
    (uncooked)
1 teaspoon salt
1 teaspoon freshly ground
    black pepper
2 1/4 cups hot water

$\mathcal{F}$ish and shellfish are easy to cook and take almost no time. I think the reason people make mistakes in seafood cookery is because they're nervous. Often, home cooks do not trust themselves enough to produce a wonderful, sometimes fancy meal. To that I say, trust yourselves and let go. If you do mess up, there is often a quick remedy so that none of your guests will even realize a catastrophe occurred. The great Julia Child says that you should never allow your guests to know that something went wrong in your kitchen. You simply serve the food and allow them to believe that's how it was meant to be. The only exception is a fallen soufflé, and then you serve ice cream instead!

Many people tell me they don't cook fish at home because they don't know how. Here are some guidelines. When grilling fish, start with a SUPER HOT grill that is well oiled. This prevents the fish from sticking. When sautéing, also start with a hot pan and oil. Brown the fish well on one side, flip it over, and finish it in a 350-degree oven for about five to seven minutes. This procedure results in a perfectly done fish. It is easier to cook fish by braising it on top of the stove or in the oven, because it is constantly surrounded by moisture. Even if overcooked, it may still appear moist when served in the sauce. When cooking shrimp, drop them into seasoned rapidly boiling water but do not wait for the water to start boiling again before counting the time. As soon as the shrimp turn pink, boiling water or not, they are ready. Incidentally, boiled shrimp are always better when cooked in the shell and then peeled. It's better to undercook scallops, oysters, mussels, and clams than to overcook them to the consistency of chewing gum. Fried fish is best coated in Japanese bread crumbs known as Panko®.

If you do happen to overcook—or even burn—your fish, dust off the ashes, break the fish apart with your hands, mix it with cocktail sauce, tartar sauce, or a rémoulade, and serve it in a Champagne flute with a wedge of lime, a garnish of dill, and a sprinkle of capers. No one will be the wiser. By the end of the meal, you'll have yourself believing that's how it was supposed to be! All of that aside, these FISH recipes have been tested over and over again and hopefully are foolproof. Just follow the directions and you will produce a dish that even Julia would award with her stamp of approval.

Fish

Moroccan Spiced Crab Cakes with Curry Aïoli

These are by far not traditional crab cakes, as you can tell from the name and the ingredients. They are somewhat sweet and quite surprising in flavor. I make these for my friend Celina Rios Mullan, who keeps them stored in her freezer and pulls a few out when company drops by or as a special treat for her and her husband G.E. The size you make them will depend on how you want to serve them (hors d'oeuvre, appetizer, or entrée). I particularly enjoy making them bite-size for a buffet, topped with a dollop of the aïoli.

Crab Cakes

Sort through the crab meat and remove any shell fragments. Set the crab meat aside.

Using a Robot Coupe or food processor, pulse (do not purée) the red pepper, green pepper, green onions, raisins, dates and cilantro.

Remove the mixture from the Robot Coupe to a large bowl and add the cinnamon, cumin, turmeric, ginger, cayenne pepper, paprika, salt and black pepper. Add the crab meat, bread crumbs, mayonnaise and lemon juice. (Do not overmix.) Taste and season. Form into patties using an ice cream scoop. Lay on a sheet tray lined with parchment. Freeze.

To cook, heat some butter in a sauté pan over medium-high heat, add the frozen crab cakes and sauté for about 4 minutes on each side (you can also bake them in the oven if you want, although you will not get a crust). Finish in a 350-degree oven for about 10 minutes. Serve with Curry Aïoli.

Curry Aïoli

Carefully drop the eggs into boiling water and cook for 2 minutes. Immediately run cold water over them until chilled. Crack the eggs and scoop out into a food processor or blender.

Add the water, garlic, lemon juice, vinegar, mustard, salt, pepper and curry powder. Purée for about 2 minutes or until light and fluffy.

Finally, drizzle in the peanut oil and olive oil very slowly until an emulsion has been formed.

Taste and adjust seasonings if necessary.

Refrigerate until needed.

MAKES 15 TO 20 CRAB CAKES

Crab Cakes

2 pounds lump crab meat, flaked
1/2 red bell pepper
1/2 green bell pepper
3 green onions
1/4 cup raisins
1/4 cup dates
Large handful cilantro leaves
1 tablespoon cinnamon
1 tablespoon cumin
1 teaspoon turmeric
1/2 teaspoon ginger
Dash of cayenne pepper
1 teaspoon paprika
1 teaspoon salt
1 teaspoon freshly ground
   black pepper
1 cup bread crumbs
1/4 cup mayonnaise
Juice of 1 lemon
Butter

Curry Aïoli

2 eggs
1 tablespoon water
5 garlic cloves
Juice of 1 lemon
2 tablespoons apple cider vinegar
1 teaspoon mustard
1 teaspoon salt
1 teaspoon freshly ground
   black pepper
1 tablespoon curry powder
1 cup peanut oil
1 cup olive oil

Vodka Martini Steamed Mussels

While working as the chef in a small boutique hotel on the San Antonio River, a group of executives from a national liquor company was staying with us for a regional meeting. One of the things they requested was that I would do a hands-on cooking class for them using their spirits. Creating about five stations, I designed a full meal that included one of their products in each dish. One of the recipes was for Martini Steamed Mussels! I must admit that the finished product was much better than anticipated and did not make it to the dinner table, as people kept eating them right out of the pot! Mussels are easy to prepare. Make sure that they are fresh. For a stunning presentation, serve this dish in one of those large novelty martini glasses.

Ingredients

3/4 cup vodka
2 tablespoons dry vermouth
Zest of 1 lemon
1/4 cup olive juice
1 shallot, minced
2 garlic cloves, minced
1 teaspoon salt
1 teaspoon freshly ground
   black pepper
2 pounds fresh mussels, cleaned
8 tablespoons (1 stick) butter
Chopped olives

In a large pot, combine the vodka, vermouth, lemon zest, olive juice, shallot, garlic, salt and pepper. Bring to a simmer. Add the mussels, cover and steam for 3 minutes or until the mussels have opened. Remove the mussels to a large serving bowl (discard any mussels that did not open).

Whisk the butter into the cooking liquid over low heat. Pour the hot liquid over the mussels and garnish with chopped olives. Serve immediately.

Mini Crayfish Tostadas with Avocado & Corn

This is a great item to serve at a party or as part of a buffet. Use larger tortillas and serve these tostadas to your family with some Mexican rice for dinner. Make this recipe your own by adding different ingredients to it. For example, spread refried beans on the tortilla shells first. You could even serve them warm with melted cheese on top. If you don't like, or can't find, crayfish, try using shrimp.

In a bowl, combine the avocados, corn kernels, lime juice, cilantro, jalapeño chile, red onion and salt. Set aside in the refrigerator.

In another bowl, mix the tomatoes, onion, jalapeño chile and a little chopped cilantro. Season with salt. Set the Pico de Gallo aside in the refrigerator.

Assembly

Divide the avocado mixture among the fried tortilla shells. Top with the crayfish and place on a serving platter. Sprinkle with the Pico de Gallo and chopped cilantro. Serve immediately and be prepared to make more!!

MAKES SIXTEEN TO TWENTY

Tostadas

4 avocados, diced
Kernels of 2 ears of corn
Juice of 1 lime
1/2 bunch cilantro, chopped
2 fresh jalapeño chiles, thinly sliced
1/2 red onion, diced
Salt to taste
16 to 20 (3-inch) fried corn tortillas
1 pound cooked crayfish tails

Pico de Gallo

3 tomatoes, diced
1/2 white onion, diced
1 jalapeño chile, diced
Cilantro, chopped
Salt to taste

Scallops in a Whiskey Cream Sauce

This is one dish where I don't follow my personal rule of no potatoes with seafood. Mashed potatoes make the perfect base for the scallops.

Combine the butter and stock in a medium-sized pan over high heat and bring to a boil. Whisk in the flour followed by the cream. Turn the heat down to medium-high and continue cooking until the sauce has reduced to a thick consistency, stirring frequently to prevent sticking on the sides and bottom. It's ready when it heavily coats the back of a spoon without really running. Add the whiskey, salt and pepper sauce and cook for 5 more minutes. Adjust the seasonings. Finally, drop the scallops in and cook for about 7 minutes, until the scallops are tender, not rubbery. Serve over wild rice, white rice or mashed potatoes.

SERVES FOUR

Ingredients

2 tablespoons butter
2 cups fish stock or clam juice
2 tablespoons flour
1 cup heavy cream
2 tablespoons whiskey
1 teaspoon salt
1 teaspoon hot red pepper sauce (like Tabasco)
20 sea scallops

Seared Sea Scallops with a Beer Beurre Blanc

A beurre blanc is a French butter sauce made by reducing white wine to a syrupy consistency and whisking in butter at the end. Here I use the same concept but replace the wine with beer! When I make it, I use Negra Modelo®, which is dark ale from Mexico. The sauce is rich and complements the scallops quite nicely. You can use this sauce for other items besides scallops. I enjoy it on steak.

Beer Beurre Blanc

1 (12-ounce) bottle dark beer
1 shallot, chopped
2 ounces heavy cream
1/2 cup barbecue sauce
1 pound butter, cubed and
   softened

Scallops

30 large sea scallops
1/4 cup extra-virgin olive oil
1 teaspoon salt
1 teaspoon freshly ground
   black pepper
2 tablespoons extra-virgin
   olive oil

Beer Beurre Blanc

Place the beer and shallot in a sauce pot and bring to a boil. Boil until reduced to approximately 4 ounces. Add the cream and continue to let it reduce for 7 minutes. Add the barbecue sauce. Cook for another 5 minutes. Place in a blender and carefully turn it on. With the motor running, add the butter a little at a time until all the butter is used. BE CAREFUL not to break the sauce. (This can also be done by hand with a wire whisk.) Keep warm in a water bath. Seasonings may need to be adjusted.

Scallops

Heat a large sauté pan over a high flame. Toss the scallops with 1/4 cup olive oil, salt and pepper. Add 2 tablespoons olive oil to the sauté pan and heat to smoking. Place the scallops in the pan, flat side down, and cook for 3 minutes, turn over and cook for 2 more minutes. If your pan is too small, do this in 2 batches.

Divide the scallops among the plates and top with the Beer Beurre Blanc.

Smoked Shrimp on Cilantro-Flavored Croutons with a Chile Chipotle Butter Sauce

This was another creation I developed to help the Dairy Association promote butter. They thought it was too difficult and opted for some other recipes I wrote. You be the judge. I think it's a little time-consuming but not unmanageable.

SERVES FOUR

Smoked Shrimp

In a shallow container, mix the tequila, olive oil, shallot, lime juice, garlic, honey, cumin, chili powder, salt and pepper. Place peeled shrimp in this marinade and refrigerate for 5 to 10 hours.

To smoke the shrimp, soak the wood chips in water and drain. Place the wood chips over the hot charcoal in a smoker or barbecue pit. Set the shrimp on a rack above the charcoal, close the lid and allow the shrimp to cook/smoke for about 5 to 7 minutes or until the shrimp are fully cooked. Remove the smoked shrimp from the smoking device, cool and refrigerate.

Croutons

Slice the baguette into 1/4-inch slices. Place the butter and the cilantro in a food processor. Purée until smooth. Spread the butter on the baguette slices and bake in a 350-degree oven until crisp.

Chipotle Butter Sauce

Place the butter and chipotle chiles in a pan over medium-high heat and bring to a slow rolling boil until the butter has clarified. Place the egg yolks, lime juice and chipotle chiles from the clarified butter in a food processor (reserve the clarified butter in a hot place). Process until the yolks have almost tripled in volume. Slowly add the hot clarified butter a little at a time (making sure not to disturb the sediment on the bottom of the pan). Once all of the butter has been used, stop the processor and taste. Adjust the seasonings with salt and hold in a warm place.

Assembly

Place a shrimp on a crouton and spoon a little of the sauce over the top. Garnish with a sprig of cilantro.

Smoked Shrimp

1/2 cup tequila
1 cup olive oil
1 shallot, minced
Juice of 2 limes
2 garlic cloves, minced
1 tablespoon honey
1 teaspoon cumin
1 teaspoon chili powder
1 teaspoon salt
1 teaspoon freshly ground
    black pepper
1 pound peeled shrimp
Mesquite wood chips

Croutons

1 baguette
1/2 pound (2 sticks) butter
Leaves of 1/4 bunch cilantro

Chipotle Butter Sauce

1 pound (4 sticks) butter
3 dry chipotle chiles
4 egg yolks
1/4 cup lime juice
Salt

Beer Boiled Shrimp with Raspberry Cocktail Sauce

If you can find a raspberry-flavored or even a strawberry-flavored beer, I would highly suggest it for this recipe. The subtle flavor will complement the sauce nicely (and vice versa). Otherwise, feel free to use your favorite brand.

Beer Boiled Shrimp

1 six-pack of beer

5 garlic cloves, crushed

2 ribs celery, chopped

1 bay leaf

1 Granny Smith apple, chopped

1 red onion, peeled and chopped

1 tablespoon kosher salt

1 tablespoon coriander seeds

1 tablespoon peppercorns

4 pounds unpeeled large shrimp

Raspberry Cocktail Sauce

12 ounces sugar-free frozen
    raspberries, thawed

30 ounces ketchup

1 teaspoon salt

1 teaspoon freshly ground
    black pepper

1 teaspoon Maggi seasoning

2 teaspoons Sriracha chili
    garlic sauce

2 to 3 ounces prepared
    horseradish

2 tablespoons fresh lime juice

8 ounces tomato sauce

Beer Boiled Shrimp

Place the beer, garlic, celery, bay leaf, apple, onion and seasonings in a large covered pot over the highest heat. Bring to a boil. Boil for 6 minutes. Drop in the shrimp (do not worry about waiting for the liquid to boil again), stir and cook until the shrimp turns pink. This should not take more than 5 to 7 minutes. Drain and immediately run cold water over the shrimp until it is cold. Keep in the refrigerator until ready to serve. Serve with Raspberry Cocktail Sauce.

Raspberry Cocktail Sauce

Combine the raspberries, ketchup, salt, pepper, Maggi seasoning, garlic sauce, horseradish, lime juice and tomato sauce in a large bowl. Store in the refrigerator until ready to serve.

Sweet Corn Cakes Topped with Salad of Shrimp, Avocado & Cubed Queso Blanco with Tomatillo Vinaigrette

Serve this as a main course or as an appetizer. The finished dish is not as hard to achieve as it may seem; it just takes some time. Feel free to serve the components of this recipe separately in other dishes that you may invent. When you make the corn cakes, I suggest that you not substitute for the cream or butter—they're what make the cakes so special!

Corn Cakes

Place the masa harina, baking powder and salt in the bowl of an electric mixer with a paddle and combine well. Add the butter and continue to mix. Next add the cream and mix for 1 more minute. Finally, add the corn. Shape into cakes using an ice cream scoop. Arrange the Corn Cakes in an unlined bamboo steamer or colander over simmering water. Steam, covered, for approximately 45 minutes, turn off heat and allow to rest for 15 minutes.

Tomatillo Vinaigrette

In a food processor, blender, or by hand, purée the lime juice, garlic, onion, salt, sugar, tomatillos and serrano chiles. Once blended, slowly add the corn oil, forming an emulsion. Set aside.

Salad

Cut the shrimp into halves. Cube the cheese and place in a large bowl along with the cut shrimp, cilantro and diced avocados. Mix gently.

Assembly

Place 1 to 3 Corn Cakes on a plate. Top with the salad mixture and drizzle with the Vinaigrette, or top with salad mixture that has been tossed with the Vinaigrette. Save any extra Vinaigrette for a mixed green salad.

Corn Cakes

2 1/2 cups masa harina

1 teaspoon baking powder

1 teaspoon salt

1 cup (2 sticks) butter, softened

2 cups heavy cream

2 cups fresh or thawed frozen
  corn kernels

Tomatillo Vinaigrette

1/2 cup fresh lime juice

7 garlic cloves

3 ounces (about 1/2 cup) white
  onion

1 tablespoon salt

1 tablespoon sugar

1 pound fresh tomatillos or
  2 (11-ounce) cans tomatillos,
  drained

10 canned serrano chiles
  (or to taste)

1 cup corn oil

Salad

1 pound shrimp, boiled, peeled
  and chilled

1/2 pound queso fresco

1 bunch cilantro, coarsely chopped

4 to 6 avocados, diced

Rosemary Skewered Shrimp

SERVES FOUR TO SIX

Ingredients

2 pounds large peeled shrimp
    with tails
1/2 cup extra-virgin olive oil
2 teaspoons salt
1 tablespoon freshly ground
    black pepper
8 garlic cloves, crushed
Juice of 2 lemons
1 teaspoon paprika
8 to 12 (10-inch) rosemary stems

*The success of this shrimp hinges on using strong, almost
"stalky" rosemary stems and large shrimp. If you can't find the type of
rosemary I'm referring to, try using a metal or wooden skewer
to punch a hole through the shrimp first.*

Combine the shrimp, olive oil, salt, pepper, garlic, lemon juice and paprika in a bowl and marinate for 2 hours at room temperature. Skewer the shrimp with the rosemary stems (divided evenly). Cook on a hot grill for about 2 minutes on each side or until done.

Fried Blue Corn Dusted Catfish with Avocado-Preserved Lemon Salsa

SERVES FOUR TO SIX

Ingredients

1 pound tomatillos, husked
3 avocados
1/3 cup cilantro
2 pickled jalapeño chiles
1 teaspoon salt
1 whole Preserved Lemon
    (4 quarters) (page 115)
1 cup blue cornmeal
1 teaspoon salt
1/2 teaspoon cumin
4 to 6 boneless skinless catfish
    fillets
1 cup corn oil

*Blue cornmeal should not be all that hard to find. If you're having
trouble locating it, try a health food store. The blue gives a nice color to the
fish, but if you had to substitute for it, any cornmeal would work
(I think I would try the white one). Remember, making recipes with
Preserved Lemons takes some planning if you don't already have some in
your refrigerator (page 115). This salsa is unique and quite good, so don't
just save it for this recipe. I even enjoy it served warm with chips.*

Boil tomatillos for 5 minutes. Place in a blender or food processor along with peeled pitted avocados, cilantro, jalapeño chiles and 1 teaspoon salt. Purée. Pour into a bowl and add diced Preserved Lemon. Taste and adjust seasonings with salt if necessary. Set aside until ready to use. Combine cornmeal, 1 teaspoon salt, and cumin. Coat each catfish fillet with this mixture and set aside.

Heat the corn oil in a large skillet over a high flame until lightly smoking, about 2 minutes. Add the coated catfish fillets and fry for 4 minutes. Turn over and fry for an additional 4 minutes. Remove to paper towels and drain.

To serve, spread the salsa on a plate (you may want to warm it up a bit in the microwave) and top with the catfish fillets.

Grilled Salmon with Tarragon Aïoli

This is a nice, simple dish, with delicate flavors that are perfect for a hot summer day. It can all be made a day ahead; just let the salmon come to room temperature before serving. It makes for a good late night dinner on top of some mixed green lettuces. I find that it's a good choice when you're expecting company but are not sure of when they are due to arrive. Once you've made it, you'll see the endless possibilities.

SERVES FOUR

Grilled Salmon

Cut the salmon into manageable portions. Lightly coat with your favorite oil (use any kind of flavored or unflavored olive oil or extra-virgin olive oil, peanut oil, canola oil, etc.). Season the non-skin side of the salmon with salt, pepper, herbs and spices of your choice. Place seasoned side down on a hot grill and cook for 5 minutes. Meanwhile, season the exposed side. After the 5 minutes, flip and cook for an additional 4 minutes.

Remove from the heat and allow to cool until easy to handle. Finally, break apart with your hands into medium-sized chunks. Serve at room temperature topped with Tarragon Aïoli.

Tarragon Aïoli

Carefully drop the eggs into boiling water and cook for 2 minutes. Immediately run cold water over them until chilled. Crack the eggs and scoop out into a food processor or blender. Add the water, garlic, lemon juice, vinegar, dry mustard, salt, pepper and tarragon. Purée for about 2 minutes or until light and fluffy. Finally, drizzle in the peanut oil and olive oil very slowly until an emulsion has been formed. Taste and adjust the seasonings if necessary. Refrigerate until needed.

Grilled Salmon

1 1/2 pounds salmon fillet, skinned
Oil
Salt to taste
Coarsely ground black pepper to taste
Herbs, spices and seasonings to taste

Tarragon Aïoli

2 eggs
1 tablespoon water
5 garlic cloves
Juice of 1 lemon
2 tablespoons tarragon vinegar
1 teaspoon dry mustard
1 teaspoon salt
1 teaspoon freshly ground black pepper
Fresh tarragon leaves from 4 sprigs
1 cup peanut oil
1 cup olive oil

Salmon Terrine

Susan Spicer taught me how to make this delicious Salmon Terrine with a Truffled Crème Fraîche. It's made using what the French refer to as a panada, a binding agent made by using liquid and bread. It's not difficult to make and your guests will be quite impressed with you. It travels well, so it is easy to take to a party. For a special presentation, serve it with my Asparagus in Mignonette Sauce (page 85).

Salmon Terrine

2 shallots, minced
1 tablespoon butter
1 ounce brandy
1 cup heavy cream
Cubed bread from 1/2 baguette, crust removed
12 ounces fresh salmon
1 pound crayfish tails, cooked
1 teaspoon salt
1 teaspoon freshly ground black pepper
Freshly grated nutmeg
3 eggs
1 cup heavy cream
1 1/2 tablespoons chopped tarragon
1 1/2 tablespoons chives
1/2 teaspoon hot red pepper sauce
Truffle oil

Truffled Crème Fraîche

2 cups crème fraîche
Zest and juice of 1 lemon
1 teaspoon truffle oil
Dash of salt

Salmon Terrine

In a sauce pan, sweat the shallots in the butter. Remove from heat and add the brandy. Flame. Add 1 cup of cream and boil for 2 minutes. Pour over the cubed bread and mix well. Cool.

Cut the salmon into pieces. Place the salmon, 1/4 pound of the crayfish, the cooled bread mixture, salt, pepper and nutmeg in a food processor and purée. With the motor still running, add the eggs, 1 at a time. Scrape down the sides. With the machine on, add 1 cup of cream.

Remove to a large bowl and fold in the remainder of the crayfish, tarragon, chives and pepper sauce.

Butter a terrine mold and line with plastic wrap. Rub the bottom with a little truffle oil. Pack the mixture in tightly. Rub the top with more truffle oil and wrap tightly. Place the cover on the mold. Bake in a water bath at 350 degrees for 35 minutes. Cool overnight. Serve chilled.

(This can also be done in a loaf pan. Cover with foil.)

Truffled Crème Fraîche

Combine the crème fraîche, lemon zest and juice, truffle oil and salt in a bowl. Store in the refrigerator until needed.

Smoked Salmon & Goat Cheese Terrine Wrapped in Crispy Potatoes

This is one of only a few difficult recipes that you will find in this book. I should qualify that by saying that it's time-consuming and takes patience. The outcome is delicious and well worth the effort, as my students found when I demonstrated it at a gourmet specialty store years ago. It is perfect as an appetizer at a sit-down meal and will wow your guests.

SERVES TWELVE

Butter the inside of a terrine mold or loaf pan and line with plastic wrap. Combine butter and thyme and set aside.

Mix the goat cheese, caramelized onion, green onion tops, garlic and lemon juice. Taste and season.

To assemble, place a thin layer of smoked salmon on the bottom of the terrine mold and carefully brush with melted butter. Spread a thin layer of the goat cheese mixture on top of the salmon. Repeat this process until all of the salmon and goat cheese is used up. You should finish with salmon on top. Refrigerate overnight until set.

Drop the potatoes into boiling water for approximately 2 minutes, remove and cool under cold running water.

To assemble, slice the terrine into 1/2-inch to 3/4-inch slices. Using about 7 slices of potato, wrap them around each piece of terrine. Heat a little olive oil in a sauté pan over high heat and sauté the pieces of terrine until both sides are a nice golden brown (the size of your pan will determine how many pieces of terrine you can sauté at a time). Season with salt and pepper to taste.

Ingredients

1/2 cup (1 stick) butter, softened
1 tablespoon fresh thyme
1 pound goat cheese, crumbled
1 red onion, diced and caramelized
Tops of 1 bunch green onions, chopped
1 teaspoon minced fresh garlic
Juice of 1 lemon
1 1/2 pounds smoked salmon, thinly sliced (gravlax style)
Melted butter
5 potatoes, peeled and thinly sliced lengthwise
Olive oil
Salt to taste
Freshly ground black pepper to taste

111

Piñon Crusted Salmon Atop Tortilla Salad

The juicy salmon contrasting with the crunchy tortilla salad will drive your palate crazy with excitement when you eat this dish. Make sure that the tortilla salad is tossed together at the last minute to prevent it from becoming soggy (my mother, however, says she enjoys it the next day as well). The tortilla salad is also great topped with grilled shrimp and is extra special when accompanied by my Cilantro Shrimp (page 36). The salmon is also good by itself with some white rice.

Salmon

5 ounces pine nuts

1 teaspoon salt

1 teaspoon freshly ground black pepper

1 teaspoon ground coriander

4 tablespoons (1/2 stick) butter

2 pounds boneless skinless salmon fillets

Tortilla Salad

5 to 7 corn tortillas (various colored tortillas make this salad pretty)

1/2 cup corn oil

2 tomatoes, chopped

1/4 cup green onions, sliced

1 to 2 jalapeño chiles, minced

1/2 cup cilantro leaves

Juice of 2 limes (about 1/4 cup)

2 avocados, diced

1/2 cup fresh or frozen corn kernels

1/2 cup black beans, cooked and rinsed

2 teaspoons salt

1/2 teaspoon cumin

1 teaspoon chili powder

Salmon

Place the pine nuts, salt, pepper and coriander in a food processor. Add the butter and pulse until smooth. Spread on top of the salmon and bake in a 350-degree oven for 20 minutes.

Tortilla Salad

While the salmon is baking, cut the tortillas in half, and then cut into 1/2- to 1/4-inch strips. Fry in hot corn oil for about 3 minutes until crisp. Drain and cool on paper towels. Set aside.

Assembly

Combine the tomatoes, green onions, jalapeño chiles, cilantro, lime juice, avocados, corn and black beans in a large bowl. Season with the salt, cumin and chili powder. Place the fried tortilla strips in a large bowl and CAREFULLY toss with the tomato mixture. Serve immediately topped with the salmon.

Salmon in Gazpacho Sauce

Gazpacho, a Spanish soup traditionally served chilled, makes for a nice, soupy sauce to serve salmon in. What's especially nice about this dish is that it's a one-pot meal!

SERVES SIX TO EIGHT

In a sauce pot, combine the carrots, celery, onion, green pepper, cucumbers, garlic and clam juice. Cook over low heat until the veggies are soft. Add tomato juice, tomato sauce, bay leaf, dill weed, pepper sauce, salt and pepper. Bring to a boil. Taste and adjust the seasonings if necessary.

Carefully drop in the salmon fillets, reduce heat to low, cover and cook for about 12 minutes or until salmon is desired doneness. Discard bay leaf. Serve fillets in a bowl with the sauce.

Ingredients

1 carrot, diced
2 celery ribs, diced
1 yellow onion, diced
1 green bell pepper, diced
2 cucumbers, peeled, seeded and diced
5 garlic cloves, minced
1 cup clam juice
2 cups tomato juice
2 cups tomato sauce
1 bay leaf
1/4 cup dried dill weed
1 teaspoon to 1 tablespoon hot red pepper sauce to taste
1 teaspoon salt
1 teaspoon freshly ground black pepper
6 to 8 (6-ounce) boneless skinless salmon fillets

Sea Bass Braised in Tomatoes with Capers, Olives & Preserved Lemons

Serves Six to Eight

Sea bass has got to be one of the most delicious fish around. Its texture is rich and almost creamy. The bass shines in the sauce I present it in here. Don't be timid and reserve sea bass for a special meal in a restaurant. Here is a simple recipe that allows you to make it at home, hassle-free. Once again, I use Preserved Lemons (can you tell I like them?), which will require planning (page 115). Definitely serve this with some white rice in order to enjoy all of the extra sauce.

Ingredients

1 (28-ounce) can chopped tomatoes
2 tablespoons capers
6 ounces green olives, sliced
1/2 cup sliced green onions
1 Preserved Lemon (4 quarters) julienned (page 115)
1 teaspoon salt
1 teaspoon freshly ground black pepper
3 garlic cloves
2 teaspoons paprika
1/2 teaspoon cumin
1/3 cup chopped cilantro
1 teaspoon ginger
1/2 teaspoon turmeric
Juice of 1 lemon
2 1/2 to 3 pounds boneless skinless sea bass
Chopped Italian parsley

In a large pot, combine the tomatoes, capers, green olives, green onions, Preserved Lemon, salt, pepper, garlic, paprika, cumin, cilantro, ginger, turmeric and lemon juice. Bring to a simmer. Add the sea bass and submerge in the sauce. Place the top on the pot and continue simmering for 15 minutes. Serve garnished with the chopped Italian parsley.

Sautéed Fillet of Sole with Capers & Preserved Lemons

If you have never used Preserved Lemons in your cooking, you don't know what you are missing. They add a special flavor to many dishes. If you don't already have some in your refrigerator, they will take some planning and seven days to make. Once you've made them, though, they last in the refrigerator indefinitely, and you'll be glad you have them. When it comes to the sole in this recipe, I know that it can sometimes be hard to find. Another option would be to use grouper, orange roughy, or even tilapia.

SERVES FOUR TO SIX

Sole

Place shallot, garlic and wine in a sauce pan and boil for 12 minutes, until the wine is almost evaporated and you have a syrup left. Turn the heat to low and slowly whisk in the 8 tablespoons of softened butter, forming an emulsion. Next stir in the capers and diced Preserved Lemon. Keep over very low heat, stirring occasionally, until ready to use.

Melt 4 tablespoons butter over medium-high heat in a sauté pan. Season the sole with salt and pepper and sauté for 4 minutes. Carefully flip and sauté for another 3 minutes. Serve immediately, topped with the sauce. (Note: If your butter browns, it is okay—it adds more flavor.)

Preserved Lemons

Wash the lemons very well! Quarter them and place 6 of them in a quart container (with a tight-fitting lid), squeezing each piece as it goes in. Squeeze the juice of the last 2 and discard the rinds. Top with the salt and shake, shake, shake.

Place on your kitchen counter and occasionally shake until the salt is completely dissolved. Shake each day and rotate for 7 days. After 7 days, refrigerate.

To use, cut out the "fruit/pulp part" and discard (unless you love the flavor of salt and lemon like me, and then you can munch on it!). These will keep in your refrigerator indefinitely.

Sole

1 shallot, minced
4 garlic cloves, minced
2 cups white wine
8 tablespoons (1 stick) butter, softened
1/4 cup capers
1 whole Preserved Lemon, diced
4 tablespoons (1/2 stick) butter
2 to 2 1/2 pounds boneless skinless sole
Salt to taste
Freshly ground black pepper to taste

Preserved Lemons

8 lemons
1/2 cup kosher salt

115

Red Snapper Atop Green Lentils with Dijon Vinaigrette

SERVES FOUR TO SIX

The ingredient lists for this recipe look long, but don't be fooled; you probably have the majority of the items in your pantry. Typically, I would suggest cooking snapper with the skin on because it's easy enough to remove when eating. It adds a bit of extra flavor and often contributes to the presentation. Here, however, because the fillet is served atop rich lentils and then covered with a sauce, I thought it would be more manageable to eat without it still on. All this entrée needs is a simple mixed green salad, and you have a wonderful meal.

Lentils

1/2 pound carrots, peeled and chopped
1 medium yellow onion, diced
3 tablespoons olive oil
5 celery ribs, sliced
10 garlic cloves, minced
2 bay leaves
4 tablespoons (1/2 stick) butter
2 teaspoons salt
2 teaspoons black pepper
1 pound green lentils
6 cups water

Dijon Vinaigrette

1/2 cup Dijon mustard
1/4 cup honey
1/3 cup balsamic vinegar
2/3 cup apple cider vinegar
1 shallot
3 garlic cloves, minced
1 teaspoon salt
1 teaspoon black pepper
2 cups olive oil

Red Snapper

1 1/2 to 2 pounds boneless skinless red snapper fillets
Salt and black pepper to taste
3 tablespoons olive oil

Lentils

Sauté the carrots and onion in olive oil for 10 minutes over medium heat. Add the celery and garlic cloves and sauté for another 3 minutes. Add the bay leaves and butter and stir until the butter is melted. Add the salt and pepper and lentils and sauté for 2 minutes. Add the water and bring to a boil. Turn the heat down and simmer for 45 minutes.

Dijon Vinaigrette

Place the Dijon mustard, honey, cider and balsamic vinegars, shallot, garlic, salt and pepper in a food processor or blender and purée. Slowly add the olive oil, forming an emulsion. Set aside until ready to use.

Red Snapper

Season the snapper with salt and pepper and sauté in the olive oil for 5 minutes. Turn over and sauté for another 2 minutes.

Assembly

Place the cooked lentils on a plate, followed by the snapper. Top with the Dijon Vinaigrette.

Tilapia Veracruz Style

This recipe comes from the shores of Mexico and is probably one of the easiest fish dishes to make. I suggest serving it with white rice that is studded with peas, corn, and/or carrots.

Preheat the oven to 350 degrees. Place the fish fillets in a 13×9-inch glass baking dish or nonreactive pan and sprinkle with salt and cumin.

Heat the corn oil in a sauté pan over medium-high heat. Add the onion and cook for 1 minute. Next add the garlic and jalapeño chiles and continue cooking for 1 more minute. Add the tomatoes next and sauté for approximately 4 minutes. Finally, add the sliced olives (I like using large whole olives that I then slice into 3 pieces) and lemon juice. Taste and adjust the salt if necessary.

Pour the sauce over the seasoned fillets and bake, uncovered, for 25 minutes. Sprinkle the cilantro over the entire dish when done. Serve atop white rice or with hot corn tortillas.

SERVES FOUR TO SIX

Ingredients

4 to 6 (4-ounce) tilapia fillets
    (or other mild white fish)
Salt
Cumin
3 tablespoons corn oil
1/2 white onion (about 1 cup),
    chopped
7 garlic cloves, thinly sliced
2 jalapeño chiles, thinly sliced
    (or to taste)
3 tomatoes, chopped
1 cup green olives, sliced
Juice of 1 lemon
1 bunch cilantro, coarsely chopped

Tuna Tartare

I served this dish stuffed in ancho chiles (page 145) with a cactus sauce (Salsa de Nopal, page 151) as an appetizer at the James Beard House in New York City. The best part of making this tuna there was my friend and fellow chef, Spero Kannavos, taking me to the fish market in the wee hours of the morning so I could pick out the freshest tuna possible. That's essential when making tuna tartare—starting off with fresh, sushi-grade if possible, tuna.

Tuna

Fill a large bowl with ice and place another smaller bowl inside. Add the capers, onion, green onion tops, olive oil, Chipotle Mustard and lime juice.

On a large cutting board, using a big sharp chef's knife, cut the tuna into smaller pieces. Next, roughly chop the tuna into very small pieces (about 1/4-inch square; you don't have to be precise). This must be done slowly and methodically because you don't want to end up with mush! Place the tuna in the iced bowl and mix well. Refrigerate for 2 to 4 hours before serving.

Chipotle Mustard

Place the prepared mustard and chipotle chiles in a food processor and purée until smooth. Refrigerate.

SERVES FOUR TO SIX

Tuna

2 tablespoons chopped capers
3 tablespoons minced red onion
Tops of 2 green onions, thinly
    sliced
2 tablespoons olive oil
3 tablespoons Chipotle Mustard
Juice of 2 limes
1 pound very fresh tuna

Chipotle Mustard

8 ounces prepared mustard
2 chipotle chiles in adobo sauce

Mango-Glazed Tuna with Moroccan Guacamole

My inspiration for this dish was a hoisin-glazed tuna with sesame guacamole that I enjoyed at Bayona when they celebrated their fifth anniversary. I liked the concept and wanted to create something like it at my Mediterranean restaurant. This was the result, and it is one of my favorite recipes. The tuna works best when using a very fresh, sushi-grade piece. The guacamole is another one of those to-die-for recipes. Don't expect, however, a taste similar to what you'll find in a Mexican restaurant; it's very different. This recipe (served with shrimp, instead of tuna) helped me win the "People's Choice Award" at the 11th annual Texas Hill Country Wine and Food Festival held in Austin, Texas.

Mango-Glazed Tuna

4 cups puréed mangoes with juice
1 cup packed dark brown sugar
1/2 cup rice vinegar
1 tablespoon ground cardamom
Dash of salt
Dash of freshly ground black
  pepper
4 to 6 (6- to 8-ounce) tuna steaks
Corn oil

Moroccan Guacamole

4 avocados
Juice of 1 lemon
1/2 cup plain yogurt
1/4 cup chopped cilantro
1/4 teaspoon ground cinnamon
1/2 teaspoon ground cumin
1/2 teaspoon ground turmeric
1/2 teaspoon minced garlic
1/2 teaspoon minced ginger
1 teaspoon salt
1 teaspoon freshly ground
  black pepper
1/8 teaspoon cayenne pepper
1/8 teaspoon ground cloves
1/4 teaspoon anise seeds
1/8 teaspoon ground allspice

Mango-Glazed Tuna

Combine the mango purée, brown sugar, vinegar and spices in a container with a top. Add the tuna and marinate in the refrigerator for 24 hours.

To cook, lightly coat the bottom of a sauté pan with some corn oil and warm over medium-high heat until you see the oil ripple. Sear the tuna on each side for about 1 to 2 minutes (watch carefully because the high-sugar marinade will burn quickly). Afterwards, place in a 325-degree oven and bake for about 3 to 5 minutes, or until the desired doneness. Serve topped with Moroccan Guacamole.

Moroccan Guacamole

Place the peeled avocados in a bowl and smash with a fork—don't make it too smooth.

Add the lemon juice, yogurt, cilantro, cinnamon, cumin, turmeric, garlic, ginger, salt, pepper, cayenne pepper, cloves, anise seeds and allspice and mix until combined. Let sit in the refrigerator for several hours to allow the flavors to develop.

Olive Oil Poached Tuna with Greek Skordalia Sauce

Skordalia, a staple of the Greek table, is a delicious, garlicky sauce. It can be made with either nuts and bread crumbs or potatoes. I have chosen the latter. It's delicious not only on this unique poached tuna, but also as an addition to vegetables, roasts, and chicken.

SERVES SIX TO EIGHT

Skordalia Sauce

Bake the potatoes in a 400-degree oven until tender, about 45 minutes or until a knife pokes in and slides out easily. Let cool until you can handle them, at which time they should be peeled and cubed.

Place the potatoes, garlic, salt, egg and vinegar in a food processor and quickly pulse to combine. With the motor running, quickly add the olive oil until combined. Serve atop the poached tuna with a heavy sprinkling of paprika for color.

Tuna

Place enough oil in a deep pan to cover the tuna (about 2 inches). Add the rosemary, oregano and garlic. Heat the oil over medium-low heat until the temperature reaches about 120 degrees. Add the tuna steaks and turn the heat to low (at this point, the temperature will drop to about 110 degrees and will probably stay there). Poach the tuna for about 4 to 5 minutes. Remove to a paper towel to drain and rest for 2 to 3 minutes..

Skordalia Sauce

1 pound baking potatoes
7 to 9 garlic cloves
1 teaspoon salt
1 egg
1/4 cup red wine vinegar
1 cup olive oil
Paprika

Tuna

Olive oil
5 (4- to 5-inch) rosemary sprigs
4 (4- to 5-inch) oregano sprigs
7 garlic cloves
6 to 8 (1-inch) boneless skinless tuna steaks

*T*his section includes recipes not only for beef and chicken but also for pork, veal, duck, quail, lamb, and hen. I want to explain about cooking times and temperatures. When roasting or braising, as long as enough moisture is present, you can let it go for a while, provided you don't get carried away. Unfortunately, determining doneness in foods cooked by dry-heat methods such as grilling or sautéing is by no means easy, nor is it a precise science. You really must cook a particular type and cut of meat over a thousand times before coming close to possessing any understanding of how it cooks. It is impossible for me to give you exact times for cooking meats and poultry. I realize that it would be really helpful to let you know that a filet mignon will be cooked rare in about five or six minutes, but this direction ignores some very important factors. For example, the heat intensity, the number of pieces being cooked, even the age of the meat and the way it was raised can affect the cooking time.

I can only provide you with some guidelines and a basic knowledge, here and in the recipes that follow. Red meats and game should be a rich, dark brown on the outside. Poultry, pork, and even veal should be more golden in color. As I hinted at in the beginning of this book under the section entitled "Getting Started," the only meat (and I use this term in the Catholic Lenten sense, meaning everything but fish!) that really needs to be thoroughly cooked until there is no pink is fowl such as chicken, Cornish hens, and quail. Pork can be served slightly pink and duck can be cooked and served at temperatures representative of a juicy steak. And of course we all know that beef and lamb can be served anywhere from the still "moooooing" stage to that of a charcoal briquette.

Remember, if you like meat rare, eat it cooked that way. If you prefer it well done, like my father does, go for it. Do not be intimidated from cooking your meat until charred or feeling that you cannot order it well done in a restaurant. As I have said before, food is to be enjoyed. If it doesn't tickle your palate and happily fill your stomach, what's the purpose? It is your palate, your experience, and your enjoyment that is at stake.

I do have a hint to use when trying to determine the doneness of any of the items in this MEAT & POULTRY section. It's a trick that I use even with all of the experience under my toque. Choose the piece of meat that you intend to serve to yourself. Flip it over to the bottom and cut into it to check the doneness. You may even cut it in half if you want to, as long as you serve it to yourself or someone else who knows what's going on!

And finally, if you are a vegetarian, try some of these sauces, butters, and marinades on veggies or legumes; you'll love the outcome. Just remember, no matter how you prepare these recipes, rare to well done, on sweetbreads or sweet peas, eat them to make yourself happy.

Beef · Pork · Poultry

Tamarind Cured Beef Tenderloin with a Gorgonzola Pumpkin Seed Salsa

This has become one of my signature dishes. I created it for my good friend Pat Mozersky's TV show, What's Cooking San Antonio? The original recipe was a little more involved and included stuffing the fillets with toasted garlic cloves and serrano chiles and wrapping them with Hoja Santa leaves. Next, I made it using beef tri-tip and presented the whole "roast" to the Texas Beef Council. It was also my main course for the dinner I cooked at the renowned James Beard House in New York City. For that meal, I sat it in a pool of my Beer Beurre Blanc (page 104) and topped it with the salsa. I'm sure you will enjoy it as much as everyone before you has.

SERVES FOUR TO SIX

Beef Tenderloin

Place the tenderloin in an extra-large sealable plastic bag. Add the Tamarind Beverage Base, tequila, corn oil, serrano chile and garlic. Squeeze out the air and seal. Refrigerate for 24 hours.

Gorgonzola Pumpkin Seed Salsa

Carefully combine the pumpkin seeds, vinegar, green onions, cheese, olive oil, cilantro, jalapeño chile, garlic, lime juice and salt in a bowl—do not overmix. Taste and add salt if you think it needs it. Refrigerate overnight to allow the flavors to develop (the flavor is very different the next day). Serve at room temperature.

Assembly

Remove the fillets from the marinade and discard the marinade. Season each side with salt and pepper and sauté in hot oil on each side for 3 minutes (watch the meat carefully because the marinade may burn). Finish the meat in a 350-degree oven for 4 to 10 minutes depending on the desired doneness (see notes in Getting Started). Serve the tenderloin topped with the Gorgonzola Pumpkin Seed Salsa.

Beef Tenderloin

4 to 6 (6-ounce) beef tenderloin fillets

1 (16.8-ounce) bottle Princesa® Tamarind Beverage Base (found in the ethnic food section at your grocery store or at Latin American markets)

1/4 cup tequila

1/4 cup corn oil

1 serrano chile, coarsely chopped

1 garlic clove, smashed

Gorgonzola Pumpkin Seed Salsa

1 cup pumpkin seeds, toasted

3 tablespoons sherry vinegar

2 green onions, sliced

4 ounces Gorgonzola cheese, crumbled

2 tablespoons olive oil

1 large handful cilantro leaves, chopped

1 jalapeño chile, seeded and minced

1/2 teaspoon minced garlic

Juice of 1 lime

Salt to taste

Porterhouse Steak with Eggplant & Olive Butters

Compound butters like the two used here are great on steaks. They allow a meat lover to enjoy the flavor of the beef without its getting masked by a heavy sauce. The two butter recipes below make larger amounts than needed. That's okay. Keep them in your freezer and use them on anything and everything. You'll soon find yourself making more.

SERVES TWO

Steak

1 (2½-pound) porterhouse steak
¼ cup olive oil
Salt to taste
Freshly ground black pepper
    to taste

Olive Butter

1 pound butter
2 shallots
1 cup pitted green olives
1 cup pitted kalamata olives
¼ cup Dijon mustard
2 tablespoons lemon juice
1 teaspoon freshly ground
    black pepper

Eggplant Butter

1 eggplant, peeled and diced
½ red onion, diced
½ plum tomato, peeled, seeded
    and diced
1 garlic clove, minced
1 teaspoon chopped fresh thyme
1 teaspoon chopped fresh
    oregano
1 tablespoon brown sugar
2 tablespoons balsamic vinegar
4 tablespoons sherry vinegar
1 teaspoon ginger
Salt and freshly ground black
    pepper to taste
1 pound butter, softened

Steak

Allow the steak to come to room temperature and rub with the oil, salt and pepper. Over a medium fire, cook the steak for about 10 minutes per side. During cooking, if flare-ups occur, remove the steak with long tongs, allow the fire to go down and then return the steak to the grill. Remove the steak from the fire. Allow to rest for 5 minutes and top immediately with the desired amount of the two Butters before serving.

Olive Butter

Place the butter, shallots, green and kalamata olives, Dijon mustard, lemon juice and pepper in the Robot Coupe or food processor and mix well. (Do not overprocess.) Using parchment paper, form into a log approximately 2 inches in diameter. Refrigerate or freeze. Slice off ½-inch slices as you need them.

Eggplant Butter

Place the eggplant, onion, tomato, garlic, thyme, oregano, brown sugar, balsamic vinegar, sherry vinegar, salt and pepper in a pot and cook over low heat until the vegetables are tender. Remove from heat, chill and drain all the liquid. In a mixing bowl combine the eggplant mixture and softened butter until fully incorporated. Place the eggplant butter on a piece of parchment paper and form into a log. Place in the refrigerator or freezer and chill until completely hardened. To serve, slice the butter into ½-inch disks.

Filets Mignons with Ancho Chile Garlic Crust

SERVES FOUR TO TEN

On a trip to San Miguel de Allende, Mexico, I had dinner at a popular hangout called Tio Lucas. There, I ate a fillet of beef that was seasoned with what appeared to be fresh garlic and ancho chile powder. During a conversation with the owner, I asked him what was in it, and he ignored the question. When I asked him again, he told me it was a secret. Later in the evening, before I ate my last bite, I took out my notebook and started jotting down some notes; the owner suddenly appeared out of nowhere to see what I was writing! Though nothing like what I ate that night, here is what it inspired.

Place the ancho chiles, garlic and vinegar in a pot with enough water to cover. Simmer, covered, for 35 minutes. Drain and place in a food processor with 1 teaspoon salt and purée until smooth. Set aside until ready to use.

Season the steaks with salt, pepper and cumin. Sear in hot corn oil for 3 minutes on each side. Cool until you can handle them.

Coat each filet with the ancho chile purée. Place in a baking pan that has been coated with the corn oil from the pan used for searing. Roast in a 350-degree oven until desired doneness has been achieved:

- 4 minutes for rare
- 7 minutes for medium-rare
- 9 minutes for medium-well
- 15 minutes for well-done.
  (I cheat and pull out the steak I plan to eat and cut into it from the bottom to check for doneness!)

Ingredients

5 to 7 (3-ounce) ancho chiles, stemmed and seeded
15 garlic cloves
3 tablespoons red wine vinegar
1 teaspoon salt
4 to 10 (6-ounce) filets mignons
Salt to taste
Freshly ground black pepper to taste
Cumin to taste
Corn oil

Beef Kebabs

SERVES FOUR TO SIX

Ingredients

1 1/2 to 2 pounds round, flank
    or chuck steaks, cut into
    1 1/2-inch cubes
3/4 cup olive oil
1/2 cup Sauternes
Juice of 1 lemon
1 garlic clove, minced
1 teaspoon salt
1/2 teaspoon freshly ground
    black pepper
1 medium onion, finely chopped
Salt and freshly ground black
    pepper to taste

*A Sauternes is a sweet, white dessert wine and the secret ingredient
for these kebabs. Though not in the recipe, feel free to add vegetables to
your skewers. The marinade is equally as good on brisket.*

Place the steak cubes in a large sealable plastic bag. Add the olive oil, Sauternes, lemon juice, garlic, salt, pepper and onion. Squeeze out the air and seal. Marinate in the refrigerator overnight. If using wooden skewers, they should soak in water overnight.

To assemble the kebabs, spear about 5 pieces of steak onto each skewer. Sprinkle with salt and pepper. Grill over medium heat anywhere from 6 to 12 minutes, depending on desired doneness. Turn the skewers often.

Gorgonzola Burgers

SERVES FOUR

Ingredients

1 pound lean ground beef
1 teaspoon salt
1 teaspoon freshly ground
    black pepper
3 tablespoons Worcestershire
    sauce
1/4 cup diced onion
1/4 cup canned diced tomatoes
1 egg
1 egg yolk
1/3 cup cracker crumbs
3 garlic cloves, minced
1 tablespoon capers
1 tablespoon green peppercorns
    in brine
8 ounces Gorgonzola cheese,
    cut into 4 pieces

*This gourmet hamburger is for the more discriminating backyard chef! Be
careful to seal the edges well or the cheese will run out. I also suggest letting
the patties rest for a few minutes before devouring them (if you can wait).*

Combine the ground beef, salt, pepper, Worcestershire sauce, onion, tomatoes, egg, egg yolk, cracker crumbs, garlic, capers and peppercorns in a large bowl. Divide into fourths and form hamburger patties. Cut the patties in half from side to side. Place a slice of cheese on each bottom, and then put the tops

back on, sealing well. Grill or sauté the patties for about 5 minutes on each side or until desired doneness is achieved, or roast in a 350-degree oven for about 10 minutes.

Serve on toasted hamburger buns with your favorite garnishes.

Greek Lamb Chops

Retsina is a Greek wine that has somewhat of a pine taste to it. Although it's not my favorite to drink, it makes a mouthwatering marinade for lamb.

Combine the lamb chops, retsina, olive oil, rosemary, garlic, onion, pepper, lemon juice, salt and mint in a container. The lamb must be marinated in the refrigerator for at least 12 to 24 hours before using.

To cook, remove the lamb from the marinade and grill over a medium flame for about 4 to 7 minutes per side, depending on desired doneness. Let rest for about 5 minutes before serving.

(Note: If flame flares up during cooking, pull the meat off with long tongs until the flame subsides.)

SERVES FOUR TO SIX

Ingredients
8 to 12 double-rib chops of lamb
1 cup retsina
2 cups olive oil
1 (2/3-ounce) bunch rosemary
1/4 cup minced garlic
1/2 yellow onion, coarsely chopped
1 tablespoon black pepper
Juice of 1 lemon
1 tablespoon salt
1 (2/3-ounce) bunch mint

Hoisin-Glazed Lamb

The marinade here is also good on pork chops. Try both served with vegetable fried rice (homemade or takeout, it doesn't matter). Leftover aïoli makes a great tuna salad.

Lamb and Hoisin Marinade
Combine the hoisin sauce, vinegar, soy sauce and sambal oelek in a bowl. Add the lamb and marinate in the refrigerator for 12 to 24 hours.

Preheat the oven to 350 degrees. Arrange the lamb chops on a baking sheet and roast in the oven for 10 to 20 minutes, depending on the doneness desired.

Chipotle Aïoli
Place the eggs, lime juice, garlic and chipotle chiles in a food processor and purée. With the motor running, slowly pour in the olive oil, forming an emulsion. Season with salt to taste. Store in the refrigerator.

Assembly
Arrange the lamb on 4 plates. Serve with mashed potatoes. Garnish with vegetables of choice, chopped peanuts and cilantro, and Chipotle Aïoli.

SERVES FOUR

Lamb and Hoisin Marinade
10 ounces hoisin sauce
1/2 cup rice vinegar
1/4 cup mushroom soy sauce or
    regular soy sauce
2 tablespoons sambal oelek
3 racks of lamb, cut between
    the bones

Chipotle Aïoli
1 egg
1 egg yolk
Juice of 1 lime
3 garlic cloves
2 chipotle chiles in adobo sauce
2 cups olive oil
Salt to taste

Assembly
Chopped peanuts and cilantro

Stuffed Pork Roast

My best advice to you for this recipe is that if you are unsure about butterflying the roast, ask your butcher to do it (tell him you want it about 1/2 inch thick). Although the thought is intimidating, it's not at all that complicated to do; it just requires some practice. For a more juicy roast, I suggest using beef.

Ingredients

3 pound boneless center-cut pork loin roast

Salt to taste

Freshly ground black pepper to taste

4 (6-inch) sprigs fresh oregano

5 garlic cloves, minced

3 ounces pancetta, thinly sliced

3 to 4 ounces spinach

1/2 pound extra-sharp provolone cheese, shredded

1 yellow onion, cut into thick slices

1 lemon, cut into quarters

Extra-virgin olive oil

3 tablespoons butter, softened

3 tablespoons flour

Butterfly the pork loin and pound out. Season the "inside" with salt and pepper, oregano leaves and minced garlic. Lay out the pancetta evenly; top with the spinach and then the shredded cheese. Roll tightly and tie.

Put the sliced onion and lemon on the bottom of a baking dish and top with the rolled roast. Drizzle with olive oil. Season with salt and pepper, cover and roast in a 350-degree oven for 1 1/2 hours. Uncover and continue roasting for 15 more minutes. Remove from the oven and allow to rest for 15 to 20 minutes.

While the roast is resting, combine the butter and flour in a small bowl with a wooden spoon. Strain the liquid from the roast and whisk the butter-flour mixture into the hot liquid and simmer until a sauce has been formed. Taste and adjust the seasonings if necessary. Serve the sliced roast topped with the sauce.

Grilled Pork Tenderloin with Apricot Almond Ginger Chutney

You'll notice that the majority of the "sauces" that I serve with the meats in this book are actually more marinades, salsas, butters, purées, and chutneys like this one. That's because, like in soups (see Soups and Salads opener), many traditional sauce recipes are rooted in the rich stocks that I find more difficult to make in a home kitchen—not impossible, just more difficult. That's why I chose to offer you some captivating alternatives that are a little easier to prepare. Don't worry; they will yield the same oohs and aahs that a classic bordelaise would.

SERVES EIGHT TO TEN

Apricot Chutney

Place the apricots, gingerroot, apricot nectar, onion, wine and brown sugar in a pot. Cook over a low flame until almost all of the liquid has evaporated. Lightly toast the almonds and fold in at the end.

Pork Tenderloin

Rub the tenderloins with salt and pepper and grill them over a medium fire for 12 to 15 minutes, rolling them over every 4 minutes to ensure even cooking. If you like your pork more well-done, leave it on an additional 4 to 5 minutes. Remove the tenderloins from the fire and allow them to stand for about 5 minutes before cutting them into 1/2-inch slices and topping with the Apricot Chutney.

Apricot Chutney

12 ounces dried apricots, coarsely chopped
1/2 ounce gingerroot, grated
12 ounces apricot nectar
1/2 small red onion, thinly sliced
1/2 cup white wine
1 cup packed brown sugar
1/2 cup slivered almonds

Pork Tenderloin

5 (12- to 16-ounce) pork tenderloins
Salt to taste
Freshly ground black pepper to taste

Barbecued Spareribs

Throughout this book, you have come across the name of Helen Comer. This is her simple but delicious recipe for spareribs.

Ingredients

3 to 4 pounds spareribs
1 lemon, thinly sliced
1 large onion, thinly sliced
1 cup ketchup
1/3 cup Worcestershire sauce
1 teaspoon salt
1 teaspoon chili powder
1 teaspoon hot red pepper sauce
2 cups water

Place the ribs in a shallow roasting pan, meaty side up. Cover evenly with lemon and onion slices. Roast at 450 degrees for 30 minutes. Remove from the oven and drain the juices. While the ribs are roasting, bring the ketchup, Worcestershire sauce, salt, chili powder, pepper sauce and water to a boil in a saucepan.

Turn the oven temperature to 325 degrees. Pour the ketchup mixture over the drained ribs and return them to the oven. Roast for 1 hour, basting every 15 minutes. If the sauce gets too thick, add more water.

Veal Chops with Coriander Pear Compote

SERVES FIVE TO SIX

Cattle that are butchered from the age of one day up to about fifteen weeks are sold as veal. It has a paler flesh and a more delicate flavor, though the cuts are similar to those of beef. If you can't find the rib chops, you may substitute pork chops for them. This compote, without the mustard and fresh cilantro, is quite delicious on gingerbread!

Veal Chops

5 to 6 (12- to 14-ounce) veal
    chops, at least 1 inch thick
Salt and black pepper to taste

Coriander Pear Compote

2 1/2 pounds pears (about 5),
    cored and sliced
4 tablespoons (1/2 stick) butter
1 cup packed brown sugar
3 tablespoons ground coriander
1 tablespoon Creole mustard
1 cup pear nectar
1 teaspoon each salt and pepper
1/2 cup pear brandy
1/4 cup chopped cilantro

Veal Chops

Season the lamb chops with salt and pepper. Grill over medium-low heat for 10 minutes per side. Check for doneness by cutting into the chop you plan to serve yourself! Remove from heat and allow to rest for 5 minutes before serving.

Coriander Pear Compote

Sauté the pears in the butter with the brown sugar, coriander, mustard and pear nectar for 20 minutes over low heat. Add the salt and pepper, followed by the brandy and cilantro at the last minute before topping each chop.

Pepita-Crusted Chicken Breasts Stuffed with Chorizo & Manchego Cheese with a Roasted Red Pepper Sauce

This was a popular item on one of my menus. It sounds more complicated than it is. Again, this is when being prepared really helps. The chicken can be assembled the morning you plan to serve it and cooked while your guests are at the table. The sauce can be made a couple of days in advance and reheated.

SERVES SIX

Chicken

Pound the chicken breasts until they are a little flatter and are about 1/2 inch thick. Season both sides with salt and peper. Sear the chicken breasts in hot oil in a sauté pan on the stove, or grill outside for about 2 minutes on each side. Let cool.

In a bowl, combine the cooked and cooled chorizo and the shredded Manchego cheese. Set aside.

Using a small sharp knife, cut large pockets in each of the chicken breasts and stuff them with the chorizo-cheese mixture.

Spread the Chipotle Mayonnaise on the tops of the chicken breasts and pat the pepitas into the mayonnaise. Place on a baking sheet and roast in a 350-degree oven for 25 minutes.

To serve, drizzle a little bit of the Roasted Red Pepper Sauce on the chicken breasts.

Chipotle Mayonnaise

Purée the mayonnaise and chipotle chiles in a food processor. Store in the refrigerator.

Roasted Red Pepper Sauce

Toss the red peppers in the olive oil and roast for about 30 minutes in a 350-degree oven. When they're done, purée them in a blender until smooth. Press through a fine sieve.

Chicken

6 boneless skinless chicken breasts
Salt to taste
Coarsely ground black pepper
    to taste
1 pound Mexican chorizo, casings
    removed, cooked
1 cup Manchego cheese,
    shredded
1 cup Chipotle Mayonnaise
1 1/2 cups pepitas (pumpkin
    seeds), coarsely chopped

Chipotle Mayonnaise

1 cup mayonnaise
2 chipotle chiles in adobo sauce

Roasted Red Pepper Sauce

1 1/2 pounds red bell peppers,
    stems and seeds removed
1 tablespoon extra-virgin olive oil

131

Curried Chicken Mole

SERVES FOUR TO SIX

I was not sure exactly what to call this dish. The idea was given to me by an old friend, Brother Ed Violet. For many years, he worked in some of the Marianist missions in India. When he saw the way curries were made, it reminded him of the moles from Mexico. He suggested experimenting with the two and fusing them together. Here is the result of those experiments—a great way for two cultures to meet.

Ingredients

1 cup grated unsweetened coconut

15 garlic cloves, peeled

1 (1/2-inch) piece peeled gingerroot

3 tablespoons ground coriander

1/4 teaspoon freshly ground black pepper

2 teaspoons cumin

5 to 6 (about 1 1/2 ounces) dried pasilla chiles, stems and seeds removed

2 teaspoons ground cloves

2 teaspoons cinnamon

9 ounces pepitas (pumpkin seeds)

1 large white onion

4 ounces semisweet chocolate

2 cups hot water

1/4 cup corn oil

Salt to taste

3 bone-in chicken breasts

3 bone-in chicken thighs

3 bone-in chicken drumsticks

3 cups water

In a large frying pan with no oil, roast the coconut, garlic, gingerroot, coriander, pepper, cumin, pasilla chiles, cloves and cinnamon over low heat. After 5 minutes, add the pepitas and onion. Roast for 10 more minutes, stirring constantly. After the 10 minutes are up, remove from the heat, add to a food processor and purée along with the chocolate. Add 2 cups HOT water and continue to purée until smooth. Add salt to taste.

Heat the corn oil in a large pot and add the puréed mixture. Fry over low heat for 10 minutes.

Add the chicken and bring to a simmer. Add the water and simmer, uncovered, for 45 minutes to 1 hour.

(Note: Your grocery store may have a "Pick of the Chicken" package that includes 3 each of the meaty pieces: breasts, thighs, drumsticks, or the equivalent.)

Chicken Breasts in Crema Mexicana with Corn & Poblano Chile

During a day trip to the city of Dolores Hidalgo, Mexico, I had lunch in a restaurant off the Main Plaza. There I enjoyed a chicken dish much like this one. Here again, I would not suggest substituting light or fat-free ingredients, as the outcome will be light in taste and free of flavor! My solution, if you think it's too rich . . . don't overindulge: just enjoy it once or twice a year. But do give it a try.

Season the chicken breasts with salt, pepper, cumin and chile powder. Heat the corn oil in a sauté pan over medium-high heat. Cook the chicken for 3 minutes on each side.

In a shallow pan, mix the crema, mayonnaise and corn. Bring to a simmer. Add the chicken breasts. Simmer, covered, over low heat for 20 minutes.

To serve, place the chicken breasts on a plate. Squeeze the lime juice into the sauce and stir. Pour over the chicken and garnish with the diced poblano chile.

SERVES FOUR TO SIX

Ingredients
4 to 6 boneless skinless chicken breasts
Salt to taste
Black pepper to taste
Cumin to taste
Chile powder to taste
2 tablespoons corn oil
15 ounces crema Mexicana
1 cup mayonnaise
1 cup fresh or frozen corn kernels
1 lime
1 poblano chile, diced

Walnut Sage Cornish Game Hens

I had forgotten about this recipe until my longtime friend, and second grade teacher, Sr. Alice Garcia, reminded me of it (recounting how it was one of her favorite meals enjoyed at my house). The rub for these little birds is basically a pesto. The concept also works on chicken and is especially delicious to use on your Thanksgiving turkey (if doing the latter, you may want to cover the turkey with foil at some point to prevent burning). One of my preferences is tossing it with pasta and grilled or roasted chicken.

Cornish Game Hens
Season the cavity of the game hens with salt and pepper. Carefully lift the skin of the birds and rub heavily with the Sage Purée.

Stuff each bird with a quarter of the red onion and orange, plus a bay leaf. Roast in a 350-degree oven for 1 hour and 15 minutes. Cool slightly before serving.

Sage Purée
In a food processor, blender or by hand, purée or chop the sage, walnuts, cheese, olive oil, garlic and lemon juice.

SERVES FOUR TO EIGHT

Cornish Game Hens
4 to 8 Cornish game hens
Salt to taste
Black pepper to taste
1 to 2 red onions, cut into quarters
1 to 2 oranges, cut into quarters
4 to 8 bay leaves

Sage Purée
2/3 ounce fresh sage
6 ounces walnuts
4 ounces Pecorino Romano cheese, grated
1 cup olive oil
6 garlic cloves
Juice of 1 lemon

Roast Duck in a Piloncillo Chipotle Sauce

SERVES FOUR

Piloncillo is an unrefined Mexican sugar that is shaped into a cone. One try of this recipe will keep you up nights imagining new ways to serve the sauce. Try it on goat cheese for an appetizer or over Dutch chocolate ice cream for dessert!

Roast Duck

1 (5-pound) duck
5 quarts chicken broth or stock
1 teaspoon salt
1 teaspoon freshly ground
   black pepper

Piloncillo Chipotle Sauce

12 ounces piloncillo (Mexican
   sugar cones) or dark brown
   sugar
1 to 3 chipotle chiles in adobo
   sauce
1 pint heavy cream
8 tablespoons (1 stick) butter
2 tablespoons tequila

Roast Duck

Allow the duck to sit at room temperature for about 30 minutes. Place the cleaned duck in a large pot and cover with broth. Add the salt and pepper. Bring to a boil and then reduce heat and simmer for 40 minutes (it may be necessary to place a plate over the duck in order to keep it submerged).

When finished simmering, remove the duck and allow it to drain and dry in a roasting pan for about 30 minutes. Roast in a 500-degree oven for 30 minutes. (Note: To prevent smoking, you may have to drain some of the excess fat that accumulates in the pan.)

When done, remove from the oven and allow to rest for 10 minutes before carving and serving with the Piloncillo Chipotle Sauce.

Piloncillo Chipotle Sauce

Simmer the piloncillo, chipotle chiles and cream in a deep sauce pan for 45 minutes, stirring occasionally to prevent burning.

Remove from the heat and pour into a blender (be careful, because this mixture will be very, very hot). With the motor running, slowly add the butter, followed by the tequila.

Return to the pan and hold over low heat until ready to serve.

Duck Breast with Blueberry Amontillado Sauce

Duck is a succulent bird full of flavor. In this recipe I call for boneless breasts, skin on. The easiest thing to do is call around to various meat markets and butchers to see if they carry them or if they can special order them for you. If you find that you must purchase the full case, do it (assuming there are not too many birds in the box!). You can always store them in the freezer and use them as desired. You'll be happy you did. Amontillado is a Spanish sherry that works nicely in this recipe. The sauce is delicate and a good contrast to the grilled duck breasts.

Duck Breasts

Season the duck breasts lightly with salt and pepper. Place skin side down on a grill with very low heat. Cook for about 7 minutes per side. (You have to watch the duck carefully, because the fat dropping into the fire will cause the flames to rise and possibly burn the duck. If this happens, use long tongs to move the breasts so that they are not directly over the flame, or remove them completely until the flames subside. Keep track of the time that the breasts are actually on the grill. Patience here will be greatly rewarded!)

When the breasts are nicely brown and about as firm as your palm, remove from the heat and cool for about another 7 minutes before thinly slicing and topping with Blueberry Amontillado Sauce.

Blueberry Amontillado Sauce

Strain the blueberries and reserve 1/2 cup of the juice. Set both aside.

In a medium sauce pan over high heat, bring the Amontillado to a boil. Tie the lemon zest and spices in several layers of cheesecloth and add to the Amontillado. Reduce the heat to medium-high and continue cooking until the Amontillado is reduced by half. Discard the tied spices.

Over medium heat, stir in the vegetable stock, jelly and reserved blueberry juice. Cook for another 5 minutes. Add the butter and simmer until completely melted. Place the arrowroot in a small cup and add 1 teaspoon of the sauce at a time until you have a smooth liquid. Whisk into the sauce. Cook the sauce over medium to medium-high heat, stirring occasionally, until thickened. Add the strained blueberries. Serve the sauce immediately.

Duck Breasts

8 to 10 boneless duck breasts
Freshly ground black pepper to taste
Salt to taste

Blueberry Amontillado Sauce

1 (15-ounce) can blueberries with juice or syrup
1 1/2 cups Amontillado
Zest of 1 lemon
1 cinnamon stick
1/4 teaspoon whole cloves
1/4 teaspoon whole allspice
1/3 cup vegetable broth
2 tablespoons blueberry jelly
2 tablespoons butter
1 tablespoon arrowroot

Quail with Beef Stuffing

Growing up, my Uelita (from the Spanish word Abuela, meaning grandmother) used to make a meat stuffing for her Thanksgiving turkey. The entire Flores clan loved it, and we all fought for leftovers to take home with us. The concept of a meat stuffing for a bird reminds me of a "turducken" (a turkey that has been stuffed with a duck that's been stuffed with a chicken). Here is a version of the stuffing Uelita used to make. I present it to you inside of semi-boneless quail. This, again, may take some calling around to find, but the trouble is well worth it. As mentioned in the Duck Breast with Blueberry Amontillado Sauce recipe (page 135), buy extra if you have to. If for some reason you can't find the quail, go ahead and use a whole chicken or turkey.

Quail

6 to 8 semi-boneless quail
3 tablespoons butter, softened
Salt to taste
Freshly ground black pepper
 to taste
Chili powder to taste

Beef Stuffing

3 pounds beef roast
3 garlic cloves
1 bay leaf
2 teaspoon salt
1 teaspoon freshly ground
 black pepper
1 teaspoon cumin
1 celery rib, thinly sliced
1/2 cup frozen peas, thawed
3 large dill pickles, diced
1/2 cup small green olives with
 pimentos, drained
1/2 cup pickled pearl onions,
 drained
1/4 cup corn oil
1 baking potato, peeled and cut
 into 1/4-inch pieces
1 green bell pepper, thinly sliced
3 large tomatoes, chopped

Quail

Preheat the oven to 450 degrees. Rub the quail with the softened butter and sprinkle with salt, pepper and chile powder. Fill each cavity with the Beef Stuffing.

Place on a rack in a roasting pan and roast in the oven until the quail is nicely browned and any running liquid is clear. This will take about 10 to 12 minutes.

Beef Stuffing

Cut the roast into pieces no larger than 2-inch squares. Place in a pot with the garlic and bay leaf and cover with water. Bring to a boil, reduce heat, and simmer, uncovered, for 2 hours.

After the 2 hours are up, remove from the heat and allow the beef to cool in the liquid.

Once cool, discard the bay leaf. Remove the meat to a large bowl with the garlic; reserve the liquid. Using two forks, one in each hand, shred the beef and mash the garlic. Add the salt, pepper, cumin, peas, pickles, olives and onions. Mix well and set aside.

In a large sauté pan, heat the corn oil over high heat. Add the potatoes and cook, stirring frequently, for 3 minutes. Next add the bell pepper and cook for another minute. Stir in the tomatoes and wait until the pan gets hot again. Finally add the beef mixture and fry for 2 minutes, stirring continually. Remove from the heat and taste. If you think it needs more salt, add it. Allow to cool.

Grilled Cilantro Sweetbreads

SERVES SIX TO EIGHT

I grew up eating sweetbreads that had been sprinkled with salt and pepper, thrown on a big grill, and slowly cooked until not quite charred. They were then put into a corn tortilla with sliced avocado and homemade salsa. This was a common dish served at my family's ranch when everyone gathered for special celebrations. That's all I knew of this tasty delicacy until I interned with Chef Susan Spicer at Bayona, in New Orleans. There she presented an appetizer of sautéed sweetbreads with a sherry mustard sauce. I was fascinated until one day I was asked to clean them—a job I never want to do again! If you are a fan of sweetbreads and have ever had to clean them for a special dish, you will like this recipe. Why, you ask. Because it requires no cleaning. You may want to pull off some of the membrane, but other than that, marinate them, throw them on the grill, and enjoy.

Pull any excess skin off of the sweetbreads and place them in a large sealable plastic bag.

In a blender, purée the green onions, garlic, poblano chiles, lime juice, tomatillos and 1 tablespoon salt. Pour over the sweetbreads, seal the bag and allow to marinate in the refrigerator for at least 24 hours. They can marinate for as long as 2 days.

To cook, remove the sweetbreads from the marinade and season each side with a sprinkling of salt, pepper and garlic powder; discard the marinade. Grill over low heat for 30 minutes on each side. Make sure the heat is low and watch carefully so that they do not burn. A little charring is okay, but only a little. Serve immediately in warm corn tortillas or keep in a 300-degree oven until ready to eat.

Ingredients

2 to 3 pounds sweetbreads
1 bunch green onions
10 garlic cloves
2 poblano chiles, stemmed
1 cup fresh lime juice
1 pound tomatillos, husked and rinsed
1 tablespoon salt
Salt to taste
Freshly ground black pepper to taste
Garlic powder to taste
Corn tortillas, warmed

*T*his chapter is purposely titled TEX AND MEX, not to be confused with Tex-Mex. What's the difference? The recipes contained in these next pages are not a fusion of cuisines from Texas and Mexico meeting at the border, but are specifically either Texan or Mexican. Though I was born in Albuquerque, New Mexico, I have lived almost my entire life in San Antonio, Texas. My grandparents were from Mexico and East Texas, and therein are my roots. My first food experiences came from my mother, and her food experiences came from her father, an actual chef. Until my mother was eighteen, when her father died, he did all the cooking in the house. To my understanding, this cooking was definitely southern, and definitely Texas.

This began as the smallest chapter of the book and then grew. It's the closest to my heart because it includes recipes that I so fondly remember enjoying as a child. I wanted to share them all with you. They are recipes that my mother, my grandmothers, and even our housekeeper cooked. I've also included recipes that I created as I began to discover and understand the richness of my Mexican heritage.

Unfortunately, the majority of people associate Mexican food with fajitas, crispy tacos, and chalupas. That really is not what Mexican gastronomy is about. Mexico's food is as rich and diversified as the landscape and its peoples. Its cuisine is deeply rooted in tradition and varies widely, from fresh seafood to wild game, delicious poultry, the freshest vegetables and legumes, even pastas and rich desserts. Its food ranges from simple to the sublime. I have always said that French food (that which the world seems to claim as superior) is nothing compared to the foods from interior Mexico. If you ate your way across the country, you would understand what I mean.

When it comes to Texas, we truly are a melting pot. I don't think that there is a culture that is not represented in the Lone Star State. For proof of that, one only need attend the annual "Texas Folklife Festival." The festival is an annual event produced by The University of Texas Institute of Texan Cultures at San Antonio and is directed by Jo Ann Andera and the incredible staff at the Institute. It draws crowds from all over the globe and highlights all of the cultures that make Texas the unique and great state that it is.

Many of the recipes in TEX AND MEX come from Sunday morning breakfasts with my father, Lenten meals with my grandmothers, or enchiladas made by our housekeeper, Rosa. I even included a delicious, refreshing drink from the shores of Acapulco. I am happy to say that all of the ingredients needed to make the following recipes should be readily available in your local grocery store. We've come a long way!

Tex & Mex

Beef Brisket

This is like a recipe my mother made for us when we were growing up. The beer gives it a special taste, and the aromas that fill the house all day leave you salivating in anticipation. I asked my mother what type of beer she used, and she answered, "Whatever was around." She then added, "That thing is gooood!" See for yourselves.

Combine the onion, carrots, celery, beer, tomato purée and paste, vinegar and corn syrup in a sauce pan over medium-high heat. Add the dried onions, salt, garlic, cayenne pepper, cloves, allspice and mace and simmer for 10 minutes.

Meanwhile, place the brisket in a roasting pan and sprinkle with black pepper. Pour the sauce mixture over the brisket, cover, and roast for 5 hours in a 325-degree oven.

Ingredients
1 onion, diced
2 carrots, chopped
1 celery rib, sliced
1 can of beer
1 (10³/4-ounce) can tomato purée
1 (6-ounce) can tomato paste
1/3 cup vinegar
1/2 cup corn syrup
1 tablespoon dry minced onions
1 teaspoon salt
1 teaspoon granulated garlic
1/4 teaspoon cayenne pepper
1/4 teaspoon ground cloves
1/4 teaspoon ground allspice
1/4 teaspoon mace
1 (3-pound) beef brisket
Freshly ground black pepper
    to taste

Campechana

This is a Mexican seafood cocktail. Use any of your favorite shellfish for this fare. Serve it in martini or margarita glasses garnished with a lime wedge and a sprig of cilantro and accompanied by saltine crackers.

Seafood
Select and prepare the desired combination of seafood. Mix the seafood in with the Mexican Cocktail Sauce. Place in the refrigerator for a couple of hours to allow the flavors to develop.

Mexican Cocktail Sauce
Combine the ketchup, lime juice, horseradish, tomato, onion, cilantro, serrano chile, salt and pepper in a bowl.

SERVES FOUR TO SIX

Seafood
1 to 2 pounds of your favorite cooked seafood (such as peeled boiled shrimp, raw or cooked oysters, crab, calamari, etc.)

Mexican Cocktail Sauce
2 cups ketchup
Juice of 1 lime
1 tablespoon prepared horseradish
1 large tomato, diced
1/2 white onion, diced
1/2 cup chopped cilantro
1 serrano chile, diced
Salt and black pepper to taste

Enchiladas in Ancho Chiles

MAKES ABOUT THREE DOZEN
ENCHILADAS

Growing up, we knew we were in for a treat when my mother would ask Rosa, our housekeeper, to make enchiladas. These do not compare to the quick Texas enchiladas also in this chapter. These are more traditional Mexican fare. ➤

Ancho Chile Sauce

10 ancho chiles, stems and seeds
    removed
5 garlic cloves
1 tablespoon red wine vinegar
3 cups (about) water
2 teaspoons salt

Assembly

4 cups shredded Monterey Jack
    cheese
1/2 to 1 white onion, minced
    (optional)
Corn oil
36 corn tortillas

Ancho Chile Sauce

Place the cleaned ancho chiles, garlic and vinegar in a large pot with the water. Bring to a boil, reduce the heat to medium, cover and simmer for about 35 to 45 minutes or until the chiles are very soft and tender.

Remove the chiles and garlic to a blender along with the salt and some of the cooking liquid. Purée. Keep adding liquid until you have a smooth purée that is about the thickness of tomato sauce.

Assembly

Combine 3 cups of the cheese and the onion. Set aside. To make the enchiladas, heat about 1 1/2 inches of corn oil in a sauté pan large enough to fit a tortilla over medium-high heat. To check if the oil is hot enough, dip a side of a tortilla in it; if it sizzles a lot, it is ready. Run a tortilla through the Ancho Chile Sauce and lightly shake off the excess. Drop in the hot oil and fry for about 5 seconds. Using tongs, remove to a plate and continue until you have done 12 tortillas. Remove the sauté pan from the heat.

Place a row of the cheese-onion mixture across the center of the tortilla (from left to right) and roll tightly. Place in a glass baking dish. Continue until all 12 are done. Lightly sprinkle with 1 cup of the cheese that has no onion. (A 13×9-inch pan will hold all 12. Place some along the sides if you need more space.)

Reheat the oil and continue the process until all of the tortillas are used up. Sometimes you have extra sauce left over and can make more than 36 enchiladas. (Note that after they are rolled they freeze beautifully. Defrost for 24 hours in the refrigerator.)

Bake the enchiladas in a 350-degree oven for about 10 to 15 minutes, or until the cheese is melted. Serve topped with hot Tomato Cheese Sauce.

Topped with Tomato Cheese Sauce

Rosa would spend an entire day making dozens upon dozens of these tasty treats and freeze them for later meals. Though the enchiladas are traditional, the sauce she would make for them is not; together they make the best enchiladas I've ever eaten! For another one of Rosa's special treats, try Rosa's Chile Cheese Potatoes (page 92).

Tomato Cheese Sauce

Start off by placing the tomatoes and jalapeño chiles on a hot griddle and char on all sides—this will probably take about 30 minutes and lots of patience. (The tops and bottoms are easy; the sides are a little more difficult. Consider the tomato a box, with four sides. After the tops and bottoms are done, they will be soft enough to force the tomatoes on their sides.) When done, remove each tomato and chile to a damp paper towel and wrap until cool enough to handle. Once cool enough, remove the skins and discard (this does not have to be totally perfect). Place the jalapeños in a blender with 2 teaspoons of salt and about 2 tablespoons of water and purée. Next add the tomatoes and pulse just until blended; you do not want a smooth purée. Set aside.

In a large pan, heat the corn oil. Sauté the onions and garlic for about 7 minutes over medium-low heat. Turn the heat to high and add the tomato mixture and cumin and stir well. Bring to a simmer. Reduce the heat to low, cover and simmer for about 10 minutes. Remove from the heat. Taste and adjust the seasonings with salt if necessary. Add the cheese and stir until melted. Serve on top of the enchiladas.

Tomato Cheese Sauce

5 small to medium tomatoes

2 fresh jalapeño chiles

2 teaspoons salt

2 tablespoons water

2 tablespoons corn oil

$1/2$ large white onion, sliced

2 garlic cloves, sliced

Dash of ground cumin

2 cups shredded mozzarella cheese

Nopalitos con Camarones Seco

SERVES FOUR

Cactus with dried shrimp is a very traditional Mexican dish that is almost always served during the season of Lent—when Catholics observe the practice of no meat on Fridays. This recipe was my Granny's (my mother's mother). She only used either La Costeña® or Doña Maria® brand jarred nopales. Consequently, since that's how Granny made them, so do I.

Ingredients

1 1/2 ounces whole dried shrimp
1 (15-ounce) jar nopalitos (cactus)
3 tablespoons corn oil
1/2 onion, chopped
3 garlic cloves, minced
1 serrano chile, thinly sliced
1 tablespoon chili powder
1 teaspoon ground cumin
Small handful fresh cilantro, chopped
6 eggs, whipped
Salt to taste
Corn tortillas

Boil the dried shrimp in water for about 20 minutes and drain. Meanwhile, drain the nopalitos in a colander (discard the chiles, onions and cilantro that are in the jar). Run cold water over the nopalitos and rinse very well. Cut the nopalitos into small pieces (I do it using 2 knives, running them back and forth through the cactus while they are still in the colander).

Heat the oil in a large sauté pan over medium-high heat. Add the nopalitos, onion, garlic and serrano chile and cook for 5 minutes.

Add the shrimp, chile powder, and cumin. Continue cooking for another 3 minutes.

Add the cilantro and eggs and cook until the eggs are scrambled. Taste and adjust the salt if needed. Serve in warm corn tortillas.

Chili con Carne

SERVES FOUR TO SIX

This chapter wouldn't be complete without my favorite Chili con Carne recipe. It's simple and down-home good. So enjoy, y'all!

Ingredients

2 pound lean ground meat
2 garlic cloves, minced
1 white onion, chopped
1 green bell pepper, chopped
2 teaspoons salt
1 tablespoon cumin
1 tablespoon chili powder
3 tablespoons flour
1 (8-ounce) can tomato sauce
3 to 4 cups (or more) water

Brown the meat with the garlic, onion, bell pepper, salt, cumin and chili powder over medium-high heat. Add the flour and cook for 3 more minutes. Add the tomato sauce and water.

Taste and adjust the seasonings if you find it necessary. Simmer for at least 2 hours, uncovered. You may want or need to add more water while the chili is simmering.

Stuffed Ancho Chiles

My friend Cynthia Guido shared this recipe with me the first day that I met her. We had gotten together to discuss the menu for a luncheon that she was hosting for Les Dames d'Escoffier, for which I was cooking. She suggested using these chiles. The final plate had them stuffed with guacamole atop piping hot chilaquiles. I have continued to use this recipe ever since. The chiles are easy to prepare, not very spicy, and delicious filled with just about anything. Try them with my Fresh Grilled Tuna & Artichoke Salad (page 59). By the way, when you're done with the chiles, the liquid makes a great marinade for pork.

Clean the ancho chiles by cutting a slit from the stem to the bottom of the chile. Remove all the seeds. (I find it easier to do this when wearing surgical gloves.)

Heat the corn oil in a sauté pan and fry the chiles on each side for a couple of seconds, being careful not to burn them. Set them aside to drain. Fry the onion in the same oil.

In a separate pot, bring the vinegar, orange juice, piloncillo, salt and pepper to a boil, making sure that the piloncillo completely dissolves. Turn the heat down and cook for another 5 minutes. Remove from the heat and add the chiles and onions. The chiles must marinate for at least 24 hours but can remain in the liquid indefinitely.

To serve, stuff each chile with guacamole, refried beans, chicken, crab meat, tuna, or seafood salad or whatever you think would be good!

MAKES TEN

Ingredients
10 ancho chiles
1/2 cup corn oil
1 white onion, sliced
1 cup white vinegar
1/2 cup orange juice
1 pound piloncillo (unrefined Mexican sugar)
1 teaspoon kosher salt
1/2 teaspoon freshly ground black pepper

Chef's Note
Piloncillo is an unrefined Mexican sugar that is formed into a cone by pouring it into a mold. It used to be that wooden molds were used. I am uncertain whether that is still the case. I doubt it, though. If you've recently walked into a home accent store, you have probably seen one of these old molds being used as a candelabra, seeing that they have made their way north of the border. Don't go through too much trouble searching for the piloncillo cones; dark brown sugar is a perfectly suitable alternative.

Salmon Salpicon

SERVES TEN TO TWELVE

I created this recipe for a demonstration I was giving at the Fancy Food Show in New York City. The aromas pulled people in from all over the convention center. You only need try it once to understand. Here "salpicon" is interpreted as a hash. This explains the two separate cooking times—a hash is defined as a cooked meat bound together with a sauce and sautéed.

Ingredients

2 tablespoons butter
5 garlic cloves, minced
1 red onion, minced
4 tomatoes, chopped
1/2 bunch cilantro, chopped
1 1/2 teaspoons cinnamon
1/2 teaspoon ground cloves
2 teaspoons cumin
2 teaspoons kosher salt
2 1/2 pounds boneless skinless
  salmon
2 tablespoons butter
5 garlic cloves, minced
Corn tortillas, warmed
Chipotle chile in adobo sauce

Melt 2 tablespoons butter over medium heat and sauté 5 garlic cloves in it for about 1 minute. Add the onion and cook for another minute.

Next add the tomatoes, cilantro, cinnamon, cloves, cumin and salt. Stir well and cook for another 5 minutes.

Place the salmon in the pan and cook over low heat. Cook until the salmon is done, carefully flipping it over halfway through cooking. Allow to cool in the sauce.

When the fish is cool enough, shred it with a fork or your fingers.

Heat 2 tablespoons butter in a separate skillet. When hot and bubbly, add 5 garlic cloves and sauté for about 1 minute. Add the shredded fish and sauce; cook just until heated.

Serve with warm corn tortillas and chipotle peppers in adobo sauce. Garnish with shredded cabbage and julienne of radish.

Texas Cheese Enchiladas

If you've ever eaten Mexican food in the Lone Star State, you have probably enjoyed enchiladas much like these. They are "your gooey, gravy" variety and sometimes end up being hard to get out of the pan. No problem though—cut them into squares and serve them as a casserole. A funny note here is that I learned how to make these enchiladas in Toledo, Ohio, of all places!

MAKES TWELVE ENCHILADAS

Enchilada Sauce

In a sauce pan, melt the shortening over low heat. Whisk in the flour and continue to cook until it starts to bubble.

Once it begins to "bubble," quickly stir in 6 tablespoons chili powder, cumin and garlic powder. Cook for another minute.

Stir in the tomato sauce. The paste will start really thickening up. Turn the heat down and add the water a little at a time, combining well. Allow to thicken.

Season with 4 tablespoons chili powder, cumin, garlic powder and salt to taste and set aside.

Assembly

Combine all but 2 cups of the cheese with the onion. Set aside.

Pour about 1/4 inch of corn oil into a sauté pan and heat it for 5 to 7 minutes over medium-high heat.

Using tongs, quickly dip the tortillas, 1 at a time, into the hot oil (the oil should slightly bubble when you do this). Make sure that each side has been coated.

Drain and place on a plate. Continue until all of the tortillas are done.

Dip a tortilla into the sauce, coating well. Place a row of the cheese-onion mixture down the center of the dipped tortilla and tightly roll it. Place it in a baking dish and continue this process until all of the tortillas are used up. (WARNING: THIS IS A MESSY JOB, BUT WELL WORTH IT!!)

Pour the remaining sauce over the enchiladas and sprinkle with the reserved cheese. (This can be done a day ahead and refrigerated.) Bake in a 350-degree oven for 25 to 35 minutes or until the cheese is melted and the enchiladas are thoroughly heated.

Enchilada Sauce

10 tablespoons shortening
8 tablespoons flour
6 tablespoons chili powder
1 teaspoon cumin
1/2 teaspoon garlic powder
2 tablespoons tomato sauce
4 cups water
4 tablespoons chili powder
1 teaspoon cumin
1 teaspoon garlic powder
Salt to taste

Assembly

2 pounds queso blanco or
   Monterey Jack cheese,
   shredded
1 large white onion, chopped
Corn oil
12 corn tortillas

Manchamanteles

"Tablecloth-stainer!" That's how this dish, whose roots are embedded in southern Mexico, translates. It's a wonderfully rich and complicated dish. This particular recipe was a collaborative effort between my friend Cynthia Guido and me for a cooking class we hosted entitled "Traditional Mexican Cuisine." I haven't made it for a while, but as I glance over it I am anxious to make it again.

SERVES EIGHT TO TEN

Pork

1³/4 pounds boneless pork loin
1/2 white onion, diced
6 garlic cloves
2 bay leaves
1/2 teaspoon dried oregano
5 whole cloves
5 allspice berries
2 cinnamon sticks
6 cups water
4 chicken breasts

Chile Sauce

5 ancho chiles
3 pasilla chiles
2 small tomatoes
8 garlic cloves
1/2 white onion
3 cinnamon sticks
1 teaspoon ground allspice
1 teaspoon ground cloves
1/2 teaspoon anise seeds
1 tablespoon apple cider vinegar
3 tablespoons sugar
1/4 cup lard
3 cups broth from above liquid
1 bay leaf
1/2 teaspoon Mexican oregano
Salt to taste

Assembly

1 (1/3-pound) sweet potato
1 (1/3-pound) jicama
1 plantain, peeled and sliced
3 large slices fresh pineapple
1 small package of frozen peas,
    thawed
Salt to taste

Pork

Place the pork loin, onion, garlic, bay leaves, oregano, cloves, allspice and cinnamon sticks in a large pot. Add the water and bring to a boil. Skim and reduce heat. Simmer for 25 minutes.

Add the chicken breasts and simmer for another 15 minutes. Remove the pork and chicken and set aside. Strain and reserve the broth.

Chile Sauce

Seed the ancho and pasilla chiles and remove the stems.

Toast the ancho chiles, pasilla chiles and tomatoes on a sheet pan in a 375-degree oven for 20 minutes.

Next soak the chiles in warm water until soft; skin and seed the tomatoes. Place the chiles, tomatoes, garlic, onion, cinnamon sticks, allspice, cloves, anise seeds, vinegar and sugar in a food processor or blender.

Purée until smooth. Some of the water that the chiles soaked in may need to be added to help.

Heat the lard in a large pot. Add the chile purée and fry for about 3 minutes. Mix in the broth, bay leaf and oregano. Taste and add salt to your liking.

Assembly

Peel and cut the sweet potato and jicama into 1-inch pieces.

Slice the pork loin and add to the pot along with the sweet potato and jicama. Simmer for 15 minutes, covered. Add the plantain and continue simmering for another 15 minutes. Cut the pineapple slices into 1-inch pieces and slice the chicken. Add the pineapple and sliced chicken breasts to the pot. Simmer for another 25 minutes. Stir in the peas. Taste and adjust seasonings. Serve warm.

Tamales Chiapanecos

At one point early in my career, I was hired to open and operate a cooking school and gourmet store. During this time I met Cynthia Guido, a great lady and fabulous cook. She came to work with me, and together we had some great times developing recipes, testing them, and then teaching them.

For one class we decided to have a tamalada, an event where everyone gathers to make tamales—and to gossip, of course! Here is a tamale recipe that we created. I will admit that this recipe is involved, but when you take the time to prepare them you will discover that they are ¡delicioso!

Pasilla Tomatillo Sauce

In a large skillet, lightly toast the sesame seeds. Remove and set aside. Add a tablespoon of corn oil to the skillet and toast the almonds until pale gold in color. Add the raisins, oregano, cinnamon, salt and pepper. Continue toasting the almonds for about 3 minutes; do not burn. Remove and set aside.

In the same skillet, add 1 tablespoon of corn oil. Briefly fry the cleaned and seeded ancho and pasilla chiles, remove them to a bowl and cover with hot water. Allow to soften.

In a blender, coarsely grind the sesame seeds and almond mixture. Remove. Purée the rehydrated chiles with a bit of the liquid to make a paste. Remove and set aside. Purée the tomatoes, tomatillos, garlic and onion; fry the mixture briefly in 1 or 2 tablespoons corn oil.

In a clean skillet with 2 tablespoons corn oil, fry the ground nut and seed mixture for 2 to 3 minutes. Add the chile paste and the cooked tomato-onion mixture along with the lemon juice and about 1 cup of the reserved broth from the meats. Simmer until thickened; adjust the seasonings.

Assembly

In this tamale, the ingredients all meet on the banana leaf. On a 9-inch square of banana leaf, spread approximately 1/3 cup of prepared masa. Place the shredded chicken and pork in a vertical line over the masa. Spoon approximately 1 tablespoon of the sauce over the meats. Arrange the prunes and olives over the sauce and fold to form the tamale. Arrange the filled tamales in a steamer and steam until done, approximately 45 minutes to an hour.

(I suggest using your favorite masa recipe or using masa harina or the Maseca® brand mix for tortillas (do not use the Maseca® brand mix for tamales) found at your local grocery store in the section where you find flour and cornmeal; use the directions on the package.)

Pasilla Tomatillo Sauce

1 tablespoon sesame seeds
1 tablespoon corn oil
1/4 cup slivered almonds
1/4 cup raisins
1 teaspoon oregano
1/2 teaspoon cinnamon
Salt and pepper to taste
1 tablespoon corn oil
4 ancho chiles, seeded
3 pasilla chiles, seeded
2 medium tomatoes
2 large tomatillos
6 garlic cloves
1 medium white onion
1 to 2 tablespoons corn oil
2 tablespoons corn oil

Assembly

Banana leaves
Juice of 1/2 lemon
1 cup (about) reserved broth
Masa prepared with reserved broth
3 cups boiled and shredded chicken breast
1 cup boiled and shredded pork shoulder or butt
Pitted prunes (4 halves per tamale)
Pitted green olives (3 halves per tamale)

149

Calabacita

Ingredients

3 tablespoons corn oil
1 1/2 to 2 pounds round steak,
    cut into 1 1/2-inch cubes
1 tablespoon salt
Dash of cumin
1 teaspoon black pepper
1/2 white onion, chopped
3 garlic cloves, sliced
1 jalapeño chile
1 large tomato, chopped
5 tatuma or calabaza squashes
1 (15 1/4-ounce) can corn, drained
Corn tortillas

Literally translated, this recipe means squash. The type of squash my Uelita (my father's mother) used when making this Calabacita was tatuma. I consider this stew-like dish Mexican comfort food. I like making it with round steak, but Uelita would also use pork or chicken for a variation.

In a deep pot, heat the corn oil over medium-high heat. Add the steak and sauté for about 7 minutes with the salt, cumin, pepper, onion, garlic and whole jalapeño chile. Stir in the tomato and cook for 3 more minutes. To prepare the squash, quarter each one and cut out the seeds (the peels can stay on). Next cut the squash into about 1 1/2- to 2-inch pieces and add to the pot. Stir well. Turn the heat to medium-low and cover. Cook for 45 minutes to an hour, stirring occasionally. The squash should be soft but not mushy. Once the squash is cooked, stir in the corn, taste and adjust the seasonings if necessary. Serve with warm corn tortillas.

Mexican Chorizo

Makes a Variable Amount

Ingredients

6 dried ancho or guajillo chiles
1 teaspoon paprika
1/4 cup chili powder
1 1/2 tablespoons salt
2 teaspoons black pepper
1 tablespoon ground cumin
7 garlic cloves, finely minced
1 1/2 teaspoons dried Mexican
    oregano
1/2 teaspoon ground cloves
1/2 teaspoon ground allspice
2 bay leaves, crushed
1/2 teaspoon ground dried
    marjoram
1/2 teaspoon ground thyme
Dash of nutmeg
1 cup apple cider vinegar
3 pounds coarsely ground pork

My childhood memories are filled with the smell of Granny's (what we called my mother's mother) chorizo frying in the kitchen on weekend mornings. After cooking this Mexican breakfast sausage, she would drain it of its grease and mix it with scrambled eggs, finally serving it in hot corn tortillas. It was the perfect thing to wake up to—Granny and her cooking! This recipe is how she taught it to me, with a few additions of my own. A hint she gave me was to fry a little up when making it so that you could test the seasonings. The nice thing about this chorizo is that you don't need casings. Divide it into 1/2-pound portions and freeze in a zipper bag. Take it out as needed.

Remove the stems from the ancho chiles, cut open and discard the seeds. Boil in water for about 25 minutes. Remove the chiles to a blender or food processor along with the paprika, chili powder, salt, pepper, cumin, garlic, oregano, cloves, allspice, bay leaves, marjoram, thyme, nutmeg and vinegar. Purée until a smooth paste is formed (add a little bit of the liquid that the chiles were boiled in if you need more liquid to help form a paste).

Place the pork in a glass bowl and mix the purée into the pork. Cover and refrigerate for 18 hours to overnight before using.

Chilaquiles de Nopal y Camarones con Huevos

(Corn Tortillas, Shrimp, White Cheese, & Mexican Cream
Cooked in a Cactus Salsa Served Over Eggs)

SERVES SIX TO EIGHT

Chilaquiles is a quickly simmered tortilla casserole that is enriched with cheese, cream, and, oftentimes, a cooked meat. I think they were invented as a way to use up stale tortillas. The idea for this recipe came from the Mexican dish Nopalitos (page 144) that I was working on for a class that I was to teach on "Foods for Lent." Trying to throw a spin on traditional nopalitos, I conjured up this new view.

Salsa de Nopal

Begin by roughly chopping the cactus and onion.

In a large bowl, toss the cactus, onion, poblano and jalapeño chiles, garlic and tomatillos with just enough corn oil to lightly coat them. Place on a baking sheet and roast on the top shelf of a 400-degree oven for 35 minutes, or until the veggies just begin to char.

Place the cilantro, salt, epazote and lime juice in a food processor or blender along with the roasted vegetables; purée. Taste and adjust the seasonings if necessary. Set aside until ready to use.

Assembly

Using a sharp knife, cut the stale tortillas (to make fresh tortillas "stale" I suggest leaving them out at room temperature overnight) in half and then into 1/2-inch strips. Next, in a large sauté pan, fry the tortilla strips in hot corn oil until crisp and slightly browned. Remove to paper towels so that they can drain. Discard the oil.

In the same sauté pan used for frying the tortillas, heat the 3 cups salsa, stock, crema, and salt until warm to the touch.

Add the shrimp, fried tortilla strips and half of the queso (cheese). Cook over medium-low heat for 15 minutes, stirring occasionally.

While the salsa-tortilla mixture is cooking, crack the eggs and mix them with a splash of crema Mexicana and salt and pepper. Cook the eggs, scrambled style, in an oiled pan until done.

Divide the eggs among plates and top with the tortilla-salsa mixture. Sprinkle the remaining queso on top and serve.

Salsa de Nopal

1 pound fresh cactus paddles
2 white onions
2 poblano chiles, seeds and
    stems removed
2 jalapeño chiles, seeds and
    stems removed
1 head of garlic, peeled
1 3/4 pounds tomatillos, husked
Corn oil
1 bunch of cilantro
2 tablespoons kosher salt
2 epazote leaves
Juice of 2 limes (about 1/4 cup)

Assembly

10 stale corn tortillas
Corn oil
3 cups Salsa de Nopal
1/2 cup vegetable stock
1/2 cup crema Mexicana
2 teaspoons kosher salt
12 ounces peeled shrimp
12 ounces queso fresco
8 eggs
1 teaspoon salt
1 teaspoon freshly ground
    black pepper

Salpicón de Res

This shredded beef salad is a delicious way of cooking flank steak. The garnishes really add to the dish's taste. Serve it on a buffet either by itself or with little rolls—or even adorn a large crisp salad with it for a unique lunch dish. It's a crowd pleaser.

Beef

1 serrano chile
2 pounds flank steak, trimmed and cut into 2-inch squares
3 garlic cloves
2 bay leaves
1 teaspoon dried Mexican oregano
1/2 teaspoon pepper
1 teaspoon kosher salt
1 white onion, diced
1 pound red potatoes, unpeeled, scrubbed
2 garlic cloves, minced
2 pickled serrano chiles, sliced
3 tomatoes, diced

Vinaigrette

1 cup olive oil
1/3 cup cider vinegar
1 teaspoon kosher salt
1/2 teaspoon freshly ground black pepper

Garnish

Chipotle chile in adobo sauce
Julienned radishes
Crumbled queso fresco or feta cheese
Avocados, diced

Beef

In a large pot, combine the serrano chile, flank steak, garlic, bay leaves, Mexican oregano, pepper, salt and half of the diced onion. Add water to cover. Bring to a boil and then simmer for about 2 hours or until the steak is tender, skimming occasionally. If you have the time, allow the steak to cool in the broth. Drain and discard all but the steak. Shred the steak.

While the steak is cooking, place the potatoes in a small pot and cover with salted water. Cook until a knife slides in and out of the potato easily, approximately 25 minutes. Cool under cold running water; then dice and add to the meat mixture along with the remaining onion, minced garlic, pickled serrano chiles and tomatoes. Toss with the Vinaigrette, and let sit in the refrigerator for 6 hours to overnight. Taste and adjust the seasonings. Refrigerate until needed. Serve topped with the optional garnishes.

Vinaigrette

Combine the olive oil, vinegar, salt and pepper in a bowl and whisk well.

Sloppy Joes

What makes these Sloppy Joes so special, you ask? My mother would come home after working all day and make them from scratch. The four of us (my father, mother, brother, and I) would sit down together and, after the dinner prayer, enjoy them as we shared with each other what had happened in our lives that day. Enough said!

Sloppy Joe Sauce
Mix the tomato purée, tomato paste, vinegar and corn syrup together. Add the dried onion, salt, granulated garlic, cayenne pepper, cloves, allspice and mace in a bowl and set aside.

Ground Beef
Cook the ground beef with the onion, salt, paprika and chili powder over medium-high heat in a large pan until browned.

Next add the brown sugar, mustard, Sloppy Joe Sauce, ketchup, pepper sauce and Worcestershire sauce and cook over low heat for 30 minutes.

Serve on toasted hamburger buns with pickles and onions.

Sloppy Joe Sauce
1 (10¾-ounce) can tomato purée
1 (6-ounce) can tomato paste
1/3 cup vinegar
1/2 cup corn syrup
1 tablespoon dried minced onion
1 teaspoon salt
1 teaspoon granulated garlic
1/4 teaspoon cayenne pepper
1/4 teaspoon ground cloves
1/4 teaspoon ground allspice
1/4 teaspoon mace

Ground Beef
2 pounds lean ground beef
1 medium yellow onion, diced
1 teaspoon salt
2 teaspoons paprika
1/4 cup chili powder
1 tablespoon brown sugar
1/4 cup prepared mustard
Sloppy Joe Sauce
1/2 cup ketchup
1 teaspoon hot red pepper sauce
2 tablespoons Worcestershire sauce
Hamburger buns
Pickle slices
Red onion slices

Chicken-Fried Steak with Mushroom Cream Sauce

SERVES SIX

Steak

1 1/2 pounds ground beef
   (or any ground meat)
1 teaspoon salt
1 teaspoon freshly ground
   black pepper
1/2 teaspoon garlic powder
1 tablespoon minced onion
1 tablespoon minced celery
1 egg
2 tablespoons Worcestershire
   sauce
1/4 cup plain bread crumbs
1 cup flour
1 teaspoon salt
1/4 teaspoon cayenne pepper
1 cup buttermilk
1 pound lard

Mushroom Cream Gravy

1/4 cup (1/2 stick) butter
1 tablespoon diced onion
1/4 cup flour
5 cups milk
Salt to taste
White pepper to taste
Pinch of fresh nutmeg
2 tablespoons butter
2 cups fresh button mushrooms,
   sliced
1 teaspoon salt
1 teaspoon white pepper
8 ounces sour cream

My brother Tommy loves chicken-fried steak. His favorite is the one that Chef Matt Martinez makes out of ground venison and serves at his restaurant called Matt's No Place in Dallas, Texas. I actually like the idea of making chicken-fried steak out of ground meat because what has always turned me off about this Texas dish is the chewing of the tough meat. I typically can't finish it because my jaw is sore. That's not the case with this one, which is similar to the one Matt makes.

Steak

In a large bowl, mix the ground beef, salt, pepper, garlic powder, onion, celery, egg and Worcestershire sauce. Add the bread crumbs a little at a time until the mixture comes together. Divide into 6 patties, not quite an inch thick.

Combine the flour, salt and cayenne pepper on a dinner plate. Pour the buttermilk into a large bowl. Heat the lard in a large sauté pan over medium-high heat. While the lard is getting hot, dredge the patties in the flour mixture, then the buttermilk, and then the flour again. When the lard is hot enough for frying, add the flour-coated meat and fry for about 3 to 4 minutes per side. Serve topped with Mushroom Cream Gravy.

Mushroom Cream Gravy

Melt 1/4 cup butter in a sauce pan. Add the onion and cook until translucent. Add the flour and continue cooking over low heat, stirring frequently, for about 8 minutes. (Be careful not to brown the onions or the flour.) Slowly whisk in the milk until well-incorporated. Simmer for 45 minutes or until thick, stirring often. Season to taste with salt and pepper. Add the nutmeg.

Melt 2 tablespoons butter in a sauté pan over medium-high heat. Cook the mushrooms with salt and pepper to taste until tender. Taste and adjust the seasonings. Stir the mushrooms and sour cream into the gravy.

Carnitas

Here's another one of Dad's Sunday morning specialties (see Migas, page 156). He usually serves these tasty pieces of pork with refried beans that have been cooked in some of the meat drippings.

(see Migas, page 156)

SERVES SIX TO EIGHT

Cube the pork no larger than 3/4 inch. Toss with the salt, pepper and garlic powder. Melt the lard in a skillet over high heat. Add the pork and stir until well-coated. Continue cooking on high for 15 minutes or until golden brown. Stir in the cayenne pepper.

Step back and pour in the very hot water. Stir. Using a spatula, scrape the bottom of the pan, loosening all of the "stuff" from the bottom of the pan. Once the water has evaporated, cover and reduce the heat to low. Continue cooking for at least 25 more minutes. The pork can be cooked longer if needed. Drain on a paper towel before serving.

Ingredients

1 1/2 to 2 pounds boneless pork
  sirloin chops
1 1/2 teaspoons salt
1 tablespoon freshly ground
  black pepper
1 teaspoon garlic powder
1/4 to 1/3 cup lard
Dash of cayenne pepper
1/3 cup very hot water

Chilaquiles

Chilaquiles is another dish that I would definitely call Mexican comfort food. This simmered tortilla and cheese casserole is one of my favorites and is good served morning, noon, or night.

SERVES FOUR

Cut the tortillas in half and then roughly into 1-inch strips. (I know that this is a little difficult because of the "roughness/ staleness" of the tortillas, but please note that this is not chemistry! Do the best you can, not worrying whether it is perfect or not.)

In a large sauté pan, heat the corn oil over high heat. Add the tortillas and fry until light golden. Drain the oil and add the salsa, crema and stock. Simmer together for 10 to 15 minutes or until the liquid has been absorbed by the tortillas.

Turn the heat off and stir in the queso (cheese). Taste and season with salt if necessary. Serve piping hot topped with the onion rings and garnished with refried beans.

(Note: As a last resort, crème fraîche or sour cream may be substituted for crema Mexicana.)

Ingredients

7 stale corn tortillas
1/3 cup corn oil
1 1/2 cups red or green salsa
1/4 cup crema Mexicana
1/2 cup chicken or vegetable stock
1 cup shredded queso blanco or
  Monterey Jack cheese
Salt to taste
Thinly sliced onion rings

Migas

This is my father's favorite Sunday morning breakfast. It's a simple recipe, but you wouldn't know it by the looks of the kitchen when he's finished making the Migas! Although he's a good cook in his own right, my mother and I still have to sneak in behind him and add the salt. It's not that he shouldn't be eating it; he just doesn't use it. Possibly what's happened is that my mother and I have secretly been adding it for so long now that he thinks it just happens! The difference between this recipe and his is that he uses a nonfat cooking spray, only egg whites, and very little cheese. When you make these Migas, I suggest cutting the tortilla strips the night before and leaving them on your counter until morning to harden up some.

Ingredients

9 corn tortillas
4 tablespoons corn oil
1 small white onion, chopped
5 garlic cloves, coarsely chopped
1 to 2 jalapeño chiles, seeds and stems removed, chopped
5 to 6 tomatoes, seeds removed, chopped
1 tablespoon salt
6 eggs, whipped
1 cup shredded yellow cheese
1 cup shredded Monterey Jack cheese
Cilantro for garnish

Cut the tortillas into thirds and then into 1-inch-wide strips. Place in a large bowl and leave out at room temperature overnight.

Heat the corn oil in a large sauté pan until hot. Add the tortilla strips, onion, garlic and jalapeño chiles. Cook, stirring occasionally, for 5 minutes. Add the tomatoes and salt, stir and cook 3 more minutes. Stir in the eggs and cook until done (the eggs should be dry). Top with the cheeses and bake in a 350-degree oven for about 10 minutes or until the cheese is completely melted. Serve garnished with chopped cilantro.

Pralines

My mother used to make these delicious pralines for me and my brother to give as gifts to our teachers at Christmas. This recipe only works when the weather outside is dry. Don't even attempt them if it's raining or humid. This is another recipe that you'll want to double, because if your family is like mine they'll eat them just as quickly as they harden. Try to use fresh Texas pecans. They are the best.

MAKES ABOUT ONE DOZEN

Mix the sugar and baking soda. Add the evaporated milk and stir well. Place in a sauce pan and boil. Stir constantly. Once it is boiling, reduce the heat. The mixture will caramelize. Test until the soft-ball stage has been achieved; then go 1 minute beyond. Remove from the heat. Add the butter and pecans. Mix until it gets thick. Drop onto waxed paper in mounds. Let sit until hard.

Ingredients
2 cups sugar
3/4 teaspoon baking soda
1 cup evaporated milk
1 1/2 teaspoons butter
2 to 3 cups pecans

Michalada

The Michalada is a fantastically refreshing drink that's wonderful on a hot day at the beach or swimming pool. This recipe comes from Acapulco, Mexico. I have had them served a variety of ways, but this is my favorite. Even people that aren't that wild about beer enjoy this beverage.

SERVES ONE

Start off by choosing a very large glass (I suggest a schooner). Run the lime over the rim of the glass and dip it into the kosher salt, coating the rim.

Fill the glass with crushed ice, followed by the pepper sauce, Maggi seasoning and lime juice. Pour the beer over it. If you are lucky, the entire beer will fit into the glass; if not, after every sip add some more beer to the glass.

Ingredients
Juice of 1 lime
Kosher salt
Crushed ice
2 teaspoons hot red pepper sauce (I suggest Cholula)
1 tablespoon Maggi seasoning
1 bottle pale Mexican beer

*W*ithin these last pages lie some of the simplest and most down-to-earth recipes in this book. Here you will see my basic food philosophy of simple and delicious at its best. I must confess that I did not always believe this— especially when it came to desserts. Just ask Susan Spicer. I remember being a young intern in her restaurant at Bayona in New Orleans and seeing the desserts that went out of her kitchen. One of them happened to be a cookie plate. I was shocked. I could not believe that a chef of her caliber would create and serve something so simple and basic. I even wrote this in the journal I had to keep while on externship from the Culinary Institute (a journal, incidentally, that had to be read and signed each week by Susan herself!). Well, the cookie plate I laughed at is the same cookie plate that I now think is one of the greatest ideas for a dessert, especially on a restaurant menu.

My culinary career actually began with much more complicated pâtisseries. When I was in high school, my godmother, Sr. Ernestine Trujillo, was transferred to Paris, France. I organized a going away party for her and baked a cake with the Eiffel Tower on it. Someone at the party suggested I go into the cake business (meaning later in life, I'm sure). By the end of the next day, I had designed my business cards and had them to the printers. My first business was called Michael's Cakes etc. Surprisingly, I actually had customers! The bulk of it was family in Laredo, and almost every weekend my mother and I would load up her car and drive down to Laredo to deliver goodies (I am always amazed at what a mother will do for her children). To make a long story short (for the longer version read the intro to the book), the business got too big for me to handle, and I eventually had to close down Michael's Cakes etc. I still, however, have the little metal filing box full of dessert recipes and cards with notes of what aunts and uncles like and do not like.

As my culinary career has advanced, I've come to almost dislike creating desserts. Ironically, I am credited with having co-founded an annual event centered on desserts called "Nutcracker Sweets," held in San Antonio, to benefit our local Battered Women's Shelter. Desserts are no longer my specialty because they require an exactness for which I now have little patience. I like to put a pot on the stove, throw in some things, and assume it will taste good. If it doesn't, I throw more things in until it does! You can't do that when it comes to desserts and baking. Here you have one chance and one chance only. If it works, great; if not, you throw it out and start all over again.

I have been blessed because every dessert recipe that I assumed would work, did. But I also put a lot of work and research into them. This DESSERT section is a compilation of not only my recipes, but my mother's and some of my friends'. These are not what my Uncle Fernie would refer to as "Fough! Fough! Fough!" (meaning too fancy for words). They are, for the most part, simple and delicious. Some of them may even surprise you, but none should scare you off.

Desserts

Ojarascas

(Mexican Holiday Cookies)

These simple little cookies have greeted families—mine included—during the holidays for hundreds of years. I have fond memories of going to my grandmother's house at Christmas time, first exchanging warm holiday hugs and kisses, and then devouring one cookie after another with either a glass of cold milk or a cup of hot Mexican chocolate (although because of the warm Christmas weather in Laredo, it was usually the former!). Later in the day, we went to the next grandmother's house for the same ritual. I now prepare these simple yet tasty cookies every year for the family. And bite after bite, I'm reminded of Granny and Uelita.

YIELDS ABOUT FOUR DOZEN

Boil the water and cinnamon stick until the water is reduced by half. Set aside.

Mix the flour, pecans and brown sugar together in a mixing bowl until well-incorporated.

Add the lard and combine just until the mix begins to barely come together. (Do not overmix.) Add the vanilla and slowly start adding the cinnamon tea, kneading the dough while you do. It should be moist enough to come together and should not stick to your hands; you will most likely not use all of the tea. This dough should not be overworked.

Lay the dough out on a smooth floured surface. Pat it out with your hands and then roll the dough to a 1/4-inch thickness with a rolling pin. Cut out the cookies using your favorite cookie cutter (typically these cookie shapes are simple, with not much detail).

Carefully lift the cookies with a spatula and place on a lightly greased cookie sheet. Bake at 350 degrees for approximately 10 minutes or until done. The edges should not be too brown. Let them cool slightly and firm up.

Meanwhile, mix the remaining sugar and ground cinnamon. Dust the cookies on both sides with the sugar-cinnamon mixture.

Ingredients
1 cup water
1 (3-inch) cinnamon stick
6 cups flour
2 cups ground pecans
1 cup packed brown sugar
1 pound lard
1 tablespoon vanilla extract
1 cup sugar
3 tablespoons ground cinnamon

Pineapple-Filled Cookies

Remember my friend Sue Leone from the pasta section of this book? She's back, and with a delicious cookie recipe. When writing this recipe for you, the reader, I must have called her twenty times in one night trying to understand the assembly of this cookie! Finally, at about 2:00 a.m., I got it—right before we wrote the Rigatoni with Tuna Sauce recipe (page 72). I hope that I am successful in conveying the process. They are actually quite easy and, once mastered/figured out, will probably become a staple in your household.

Cookies

2¼ cups flour
¼ teaspoon salt
2 teaspoons baking powder
½ cup shortening
½ cup cream
1 cup sugar
2 eggs, beaten
1 tablespoon milk
½ teaspoon vanilla extract

Pineapple Filling

1 (8-ounce) can crushed
  pineapple
¾ cup sugar
3 tablespoons cornstarch
¼ teaspoon salt
2 egg yolks, beaten
1 tablespoon butter

Icing

2 cups confectioners' sugar
1 teaspoon vanilla extract
2 tablespoons (or more) milk

Cookies

Sift the flour, salt and baking powder together and set aside. Combine the shortening, cream and sugar in a large bowl and beat until creamy. Add the eggs, milk and vanilla and mix well. Add the dry ingredients and mix well. Refrigerate the dough for at least 1 hour. While the dough is chilling, make the filling.

Pineapple Filling

Drain the pineapple and reserve the juice. Combine the sugar, cornstarch and salt in a small saucepan and mix well. Add water to the pineapple juice to make ¾ cup. Stir the pineapple juice gradually into the sugar mixture. Bring to a boil, stirring constantly. Boil for 1 minute and remove from the heat. Stir a small amount of the hot mixture into the beaten egg yolks; stir the egg yolks into the hot mixture. Cook over low heat until the mixture boils, stirring constantly. Remove from the the heat and beat in the pineapple and butter. Cool completely.

Assembly

Divide the dough in half. On a lightly floured surface, roll each piece into an 14×8-inch rectangle. Cut those pieces in half lengthwise (forming four 14×4-inch pieces) and place on 2 ungreased cookie sheets. Spread the Pineapple Filling down the length of each strip, about 1½ inches wide (leave about ½ inch of the dough uncovered at top and bottom). Fold the long sides over so that they meet in the middle. Pinch the short ends shut (this keeps the filling from running out of the sides and keeps the folds from opening too much during baking). Bake at 375 degrees until golden, about 15 minutes.

Icing

Blend the confectioners' sugar, vanilla and milk. (Also, you can try other extract flavors, such as almond or orange.) It should be thin, but not watery (like a glaze). Glaze the cookie rolls while still warm, not hot. When completely cool, slice into pieces no larger than ¾ inch thick.

Rum Balls

These are delicious little bite-size treats that are simple to assemble. When I make them, I usually double the batch because family and friends just gobble them up (not to mention me). Be warned, though, they do pack a punch. But what a punch it is.

MAKES FIVE DOZEN

Ingredients

1 (12-ounce) package vanilla
  wafers
1/2 cup confectioners' sugar
1 cup chopped pecans
6 ounces semisweet chocolate
1/2 cup dark rum or bourbon
1 teaspoon vanilla extract
3 tablespoons dark corn syrup
Sugar

Make fine crumbs out of the vanilla wafers by either pulsing them in a food processor or placing them in a sealable plastic bag and going over them continuously with a rolling pin. Next, add the confectioners' sugar and chopped pecans. Set aside. In a large heatproof bowl, melt the chocolate. Stir in the rum, vanilla extract and corn syrup. Stir the vanilla wafer mixture into the chocolate mixture. Let stand for 30 minutes. Roll into small balls. (I use a tiny ice cream scoop or large melon baller to keep a uniform size.) Roll in sugar.

Apple Squares

This is my mother's signature sweet. She bakes them all the time for family and friends. Numerous people have asked for the recipe, but none have turned out like my mother's do—not even mine! The finished product should be more like a dense brownie than a puffy, airy one (the way everyone's seem to turn out). At one point, my grandmother (her mother) gave up trying and added another egg, making them even fluffier and calling the recipe her own! You have no worry, though, because you have no frame of reference to compare them to. And anyway, all the ones I tasted were quite good; they just weren't Mom's. So give them a try—flat or fluffy, everyone is sure to enjoy them.

MAKES FORTY

Ingredients

1 teaspoon baking soda
1 cup peeled, cored and diced
  apples
1 cup sugar
1 cup packed brown sugar
1 teaspoon ground cinnamon
2 eggs
1 teaspoon vanilla extract
1 cup margarine, melted
2 cups flour
1 cup chopped pecans

Sprinkle the baking soda over the apples and set aside.

Mix the 2 sugars together. Next add the cinnamon, eggs, vanilla and margarine. Mix in the flour, followed by the pecans and apples.

Pour into a greased 13×9-inch pan and bake at 350 degrees for 40 minutes, or until a toothpick inserted near the center comes out clean.

White Cookies

MAKES ABOUT THREE DOZEN

Sue Leone, a friend and a great baker, handed me a sandwich bag sort of, kind of, full of these cookies one holiday season and said, "Taste these." I fell in love with them at first bite. They were right up my alley because I am a white chocolate, white cake kind of person. When it comes to dark chocolate, I can take it or leave it! While writing this book, I asked her if she would share this recipe with me. After a little prodding, she finally did. It is a very moist version of the Italian white cookie that you might find on a wedding cookie tray. When I asked Sue where the recipe came from, she told me that her mother-in-law had given her a cookbook over 28 years ago, and she found it inside of the book on a handwritten note from a friend of hers.

Cookies

1/2 cup shortening

1/2 cup (1 stick) butter

1 cup sugar

3 eggs

1 teaspoon vanilla extract

1 cup milk

4 cups flour

1 tablespoon (heaping) baking powder

1/2 teaspoon salt

White Frosting

1 tablespoon shortening

3 cups confectioners' sugar

1 tablespoon (or more) milk

Cookies

Soften the shortening and butter in the microwave. Beat in the sugar, eggs and vanilla. Add the milk and mix. Sift in the flour, baking powder and salt. Mix all the ingredients (the batter will be sticky).

Drop by the desired size spoonfuls of the dough onto an ungreased cookie sheet. The cookies can be made in a variety of sizes, from minis of less than a teaspoon to a full tablespoon. Be sure to leave enough space between cookies to allow them to spread without running together.

Bake at 350 degrees for 10 to 12 minutes. Cool before frosting. This batter can be refrigerated in a sealed plastic container for at least a week.

White Frosting

Soften the shortening in the microwave. Add the confectioners' sugar and enough milk (start with 1 tablespoon) to make spreadable and mix until the mixture is creamy and smooth.

Summer Pudding

For all of you that are into light and fat-free, this dessert is for you! If you have never indulged in Summer Pudding, you will be more than rewarded after assembling this dessert. And that's all this recipe really involves: gathering and assembling. I suggest using a store-bought angel food cake for this recipe, but you can make your own if you so desire.

Crème Fraîche

Mix the buttermilk and cream together and let sit at room temperature for 24 hours. Refrigerate.

Berry Sauce

Place the thawed berries and liqueur in a blender or food processor and purée. Sweeten with sugar to your liking.

Macerated Berry Filling

Toss berries of your choice with sugar to taste. Let them absorb the sugar for approximately 20 minutes.

Assembly

Line a deep 9-inch round pan with plastic wrap, making sure that there is plenty of extra overlap. Soak slices of the angel food cake in the berry sauce; then tightly arrange and smash them onto the bottom and sides of the pan. Pour the macerated berries into the angel food cake-lined pan. Top with more soaked slices of cake. During this entire process, it is important to make sure that the soaked angel food cake is packed in tightly—there is no need to be gentle! Bring the plastic wrap up and over the top of the completed cake and wrap tightly. Weigh down (I do this by placing an 8-inch pan on top with some heavy cans or a brick). Refrigerate overnight.

To serve, unmold onto a large flat plate. Using a serrated knife, cut into either 8 or 12 pieces. Place on plates with a dollop of crème fraîche and a sprig of mint.

Crème Fraîche

1/4 cup buttermilk
2 cups heavy cream

Berry Sauce

2 packages frozen mixed berries, thawed
2 tablespoons berry liqueur
Sugar to taste

Macerated Berry Filling

4 pints berries
Sugar to taste

Assembly

2 angel food cakes, cut into 1-inch slices
8 to 12 sprigs of mint

Mexican Chocolate Truffle Tart

This confection was baked for a television appearance I made one year promoting the Battered Women's Shelter of Bexar County's annual "Nutcracker Sweets," a gala centered around chefs and the desserts they create. I co-founded the event with Celina Rios Mullan. I had to fight the TV crew off until the segment was over. When it finally was, the tart disappeared in a matter of seconds!

SERVES EIGHT TO TWELVE

Chocolate Filling

10 ounces semisweet or
  bittersweet chocolate
  (chips or pieces)
1 1/4 cups heavy cream
2 tablespoons ground cinnamon
1 tablespoon chili powder

Chocolate Tart Shell

3 ounces unsalted butter,
  softened
1/2 cup sugar
1 teaspoon vanilla extract
Dash of salt
6 tablespoons sifted
  unsweetened cocoa powder
3/4 cup flour

Assembly

Stencil or doily
2 tablespoons unsweetened
  cocoa powder

Chocolate Filling

Place the chocolate in a medium bowl and set aside.

Bring the cream to a simmer over medium heat. Immediately pour the hot cream over the chocolate and let it stand for 30 seconds. Add the cinnamon and chili powder. Stir very gently just until the chocolate is completely melted and smooth. (Do not overmix.) Pour the mixture through a fine strainer and into the cooled tart shell. If necessary, gently shake back and forth to evenly spread the chocolate filling. Try not to use a knife or a spatula to spread.

Refrigerate for 3 to 4 hours, or until firm.

Chocolate Tart Shell

Cream together the butter, sugar, vanilla and salt until smooth.

Add 6 tablespoons cocoa powder and mix, creating a dark smooth paste. Add the flour and mix, forming the dough. Be careful not to overmix.

Place the dough on a piece of plastic wrap and press into a large flat disk with the palms of your hands. Wrap and refrigerate until you are ready to use. (Allow it to firm up.)

Remove the dough from the refrigerator and roll it out to a 1/8-inch thickness and 11 inches in diameter.

Place the dough in a 9 1/2-inch fluted tart pan. Pinch off the dough at the upper rim, making sure that there are no holes and that the dough fits snugly in the pan. Cover and refrigerate for another 30 minutes.

When ready to bake, prick the bottom of the shell with a fork. Bake the tart shell at 375 degrees for 12 to 14 minutes. Completely cool before filling.

Assembly

Before serving, center a stencil or doily over the very well-chilled tart. Using some sort of sifter, shake 2 tablespoons cocoa powder over the stencil, dispensing evenly. Carefully remove the stencil. Refrigerate in a covered container until ready to serve. Allow the tart to sit at room temperature for 30 to 40 minutes before you serve it.

Cracker "Pie"

Okay, don't laugh or think me absurd when you read this recipe! Let me explain why I've included it. When I was in the seventh grade, I took my very first cooking class. The curriculum was drawn up by Sr. Juana Villescas who was, at the time, the Principal of Mount Sacred Heart School. The class was supervised by Sr. Cecilia Rodriguez and taught by Sr. Philomena Rios, who was the chef of the school cafeteria. When the class was over, a cooking contest was held. I won first place with this recipe. So now you understand why it had to be a part of my first cookbook.

Meringue
Mix the cracker crumbs, sugar and pecans. Stiffly beat the egg whites with the cream of tartar. Fold the egg whites into the dry ingredients. Pour into a lightly buttered 13×9-inch pan. Bake at 350 degrees for 20 to 25 minutes. Cool.

Topping
Layer the pineapple, coconut and whipped cream on top. Chill.

Meringue
32 saltine crackers, crumbled
2 cups sugar
2 cups chopped pecans
6 egg whites
1 teaspoon cream of tartar

Topping
1 (20-ounce) can crushed pineapple, drained
1 (3.5-ounce) can flaked coconut
1 pint whipped cream

Chocolate Pecan Pie

Here's another one of my mother's sweet temptations: a decadent pecan pie with the addition of chocolate! If you know my mother, this recipe is no surprise. Her food groups are chocolate and chocolate with pecans! You wouldn't know it by looking at her; she must burn it off by taking care of her family. She makes this pie every Thanksgiving, but, to tell you the truth, I don't really remember what it tastes like. Before anyone gets a chance to indulge in it, my brother Tommy has already polished it off!

Preheat the oven to 350 degrees. Put the unbaked pie shell on a sheet pan. Mix the butter, brown sugar, corn syrup, eggs, egg yolk, bourbon, chocolate chips, nutmeg, vanilla and pecans in a bowl. Pour into the pie shell. Bake for 45 minutes. Allow to rest for at least for 3 hours to overnight before serving.

Ingredients
1 frozen pie shell, thawed
4 tablespoons (1/2 stick) butter, melted
1 cup packed brown sugar
1 cup dark corn syrup
4 eggs
1 egg yolk
2 tablespoons bourbon
1/2 cup semisweet chocolate chips
Dash of freshly grated nutmeg
1 teaspoon vanilla extract
1 cup chopped pecans

Berry-Citrus Cobbler

This deliciously simple cobbler will warm the hearts (and stomachs) of family and friends. For a more elegant presentation, bake it in individual ramekins.

Berry Filling

4 cups fresh berries
1 teaspoon minced lime zest
1 teaspoon minced lemon zest
1 teaspoon minced orange zest
3/4 cup sugar
1 1/2 tablespoons cornstarch

Spiced Topping

3/4 cup flour
1/4 cup rolled oats
1 cup packed brown sugar
1 teaspoon baking powder
1/2 teaspoon cinnamon
1/4 teaspoon ground cloves
1/4 teaspoon mace
1/4 teaspoon ground allspice
Dash of nutmeg
Dash of salt
1 cup evaporated milk
1 teaspoon vanilla extract
1/2 cup (1 stick) butter, melted

Berry Filling

Combine the berries and zest together in a bowl.

In a separate bowl, mix together the sugar and cornstarch.

Carefully toss together the berry mixture and the sugar mixture and set aside for at least an hour.

Spiced Topping

In a large bowl, mix together the flour, oats, brown sugar, baking powder, cinnamon, cloves, mace, allspice, nutmeg and salt.

In another bowl, combine the evaporated milk, vanilla and butter. Stir into the dry ingredients.

Assembly and Baking

Preheat the oven to 375 degrees. Pour the berry mixture into a 13×9-inch baking dish. Cover with the topping using a spatula.

Bake for 35 to 45 minutes or until the fruit bubbles and the topping is golden brown. Let the cobbler cool slightly before serving.

To serve, present the cobbler in individual bowls with whipped cream, ice cream, or warm heavy cream and a sprig of fresh mint.

Chocolate Raspberry Pots de Crème

This might just be the easiest dessert you'll ever make. I use it every time I cater a party—it's that good. The key to the success of this dessert is using Nestlé® brand semisweet chocolate chips. Trust me, it will not work with any other chocolate. It has something to do with the composition of this brand of chocolate. With that being said, enjoy, over and over again.

Put about 5 raspberries in the bottom of each Champagne flute. Place the chocolate chips, eggs, brown sugar, vanilla and Chambord in a blender. Combine the milk and heavy cream and heat in the microwave until it starts bubbling, about 2 minutes. Pour the milk mixture into the blender and immediately turn on and blend for 2 minutes. Pour equal amounts into the Champagne glasses and refrigerate overnight. To serve, top with whipped cream and garnish with raspberries and mint sprigs.

SERVES FIVE

Ingredients
1 pint raspberries
9 ounces Nestlé® semisweet chocolate chips
2 eggs
1 tablespoon brown sugar
1 teaspoon vanilla extract
1 tablespoon Chambord (raspberry liqueur)
1/2 cup milk
1/4 cup heavy cream
Whipped cream
Fresh mint sprigs

Warm Pumpkin Chilaquiles

I enjoy chilaquiles so much (pages 151 and 155) that I had to try them for dessert! I chose pumpkin because I wrote this recipe between Halloween and Thanksgiving for another television appearance. I was a little leery because I thought that it might be too much of a stretch for people's imagination. I got lots of calls afterwards from people wanting the recipe. When you prepare these sweet chilaquiles at home, I suggest doing it over coffee before your bridge or discussion club starts. If serving them at dinner, make them while the family is washing dishes. Then sit down and enjoy. The point I am trying to make is that they need to be made and eaten right away.

Cut the tortillas in half and then into 1/2-inch strips. Fry strips of the tortillas in oil and sprinkle with a mixture of the sugar and 2 tablespoons cinnamon.

In a bowl, whisk together the cream, pumpkin, vanilla, cloves, allspice, nutmeg and 1 teaspoon cinnamon. Pour into a large sauté pan and heat. Add the fried tortillas and currants. Mix well. Simmer until the mixture begins to thicken. Add the crumbled cheese and cook until melted. If it becomes too thick, add more cream. Serve immediately, garnished with the pecans and crema.

SERVES EIGHT TO TEN

Ingredients
10 corn tortillas
Oil for frying
1/4 cup sugar
2 tablespoons cinnamon
1/2 cup heavy cream
2 cups pumpkin purée
1 teaspoon vanilla extract
1 teaspoon ground cloves
1 teaspoon ground allspice
1/4 teaspoon nutmeg
1 teaspoon cinnamon
1/4 cup currants or raisins, soaked in brandy
1/2 cup crumbled asadero cheese
1/2 cup chopped pecans
Crema Mexicana or crème fraîche

Pumpkin & Goat Cheese Cake

This is usually my contribution to Thanksgiving. I like it so much I don't mind my brother eating all of the Chocolate Pecan Pie (page 167). If using an older springform pan for this recipe, you may want to wrap it with foil so that water doesn't seep in from the water bath. I make this cake late on the night before I plan to serve it. When it's done cooking, I turn off the oven and leave it there until morning. This seems to help it set.

Ingredients

1 tablespoon unsalted butter, softened

2 tablespoons sugar

1/2 cup pumpkin seeds, toasted

1/2 cup graham cracker crumbs

4 tablespoons (1/2 stick) unsalted butter, melted

32 ounces cream cheese, softened

1 1/2 cups pumpkin pie filling

12 ounces goat cheese, softened

2 eggs

2 cups packed brown sugar

1 teaspoon vanilla extract

3 tablespoons spiced rum

Preheat the oven to 350 degrees. Using 1 tablespoon butter, grease a 9-inch springform pan and then dust it with the sugar.

Pulverize the toasted pumpkin seeds in a blender or food processor. Mix with the graham cracker crumbs and melted butter, and press onto the bottom of the springform pan. Bake for 12 minutes.

In a large bowl, beat the cream cheese with an electric mixer until smooth, about 3 minutes. Next beat in the pumpkin, goat cheese, eggs and brown sugar. Continue beating until the mixture is smooth and creamy. Add the vanilla and rum and beat for another minute.

Pour the filling over the baked crust and bake for 1 1/2 hours or until bouncy in the center. Allow to cool at room temperature until ready to serve. If refrigerated, let come to room temperature before cutting with a sharp warm knife.

"Can't Get Better Than This" Chocolate Cake

I named this after one of my little brother's favorite sayings. Tommy is so even-tempered that he uses this saying a lot . . . wouldn't it be great to have his attitude?!? It's a very rich and decadent cake that is basically flourless. I also refer to it as a Chocolate Truffle Cake. One bite and you'll know why both titles are correct.

SERVES TWELVE

Preheat the oven to 350 degrees. Spray a springform pan with butter spray and line the bottom with parchment paper (spray the paper also). Wrap the pan with foil so that water from the water bath does not seep in.

Combine the chocolate, sugar and butter in a double boiler and heat until the chocolate and butter are melted and the sugar is dissolved. Stir in the vanilla.

Meanwhile, in a separate bowl, beat the eggs for about 1 minute. Next beat in the flour.

Once the chocolate mixture has melted, slowly beat it into the egg mixture until well-blended. Pour into the prepared pan.

Place the foil-wrapped pan in a hot water bath that goes at least 3/4 of the way up the pan. Bake for 25 to 30 minutes or until the edge of the cake is set but the center is still soft. Cool before removing from the pan.

Cut with a sharp knife that has been dipped in HOT water. Garnish with confectioners' sugar if desired.

Ingredients

9 ounces semisweet chocolate
1/2 cup sugar
1 cup (2 sticks) butter
1 tablespoon Mexican vanilla
5 eggs
1 tablespoon flour

Chocolate Bread

This recipe is a source of joy if you happen to be a bread baker that loves chocolate. It's ideal for a hostess gift or housewarming gift. I use it to make toasted Brie sandwiches, and yummy French toast.

Ingredients

1 envelope active dry yeast, or
   1 (17-gram) cake compressed
   yeast
1/2 teaspoon sugar
1/3 cup warm water
4 1/2 cups flour
6 tablespoons brown sugar
1/3 cup Dutch process cocoa
   powder
2 teaspoons salt
6 ounces semisweet chocolate
   chips
1 teaspoon vanilla extract
1 1/4 cups warm water
2 egg yolks
1 tablespoon butter, softened

Stir the yeast, sugar and 1/3 cup water in a large bowl. Let stand until foamy, about 12 minutes.

Mix the flour, brown sugar, cocoa powder, salt and chocolate chips in a separate bowl.

To the bowl that has the yeast, add the vanilla, 1 1/4 cups warm water, egg yolks and butter. Add the flour mixture to the the yeast mixture and stir with a wooden spoon. When it gets too hard to mix with the spoon, dump the mixture out onto a floured surface and knead by hand for 5 to 7 minutes, dusting with flour as needed. Or, mix in the bowl of an electric mixer fitted with the paddle attachment. Stir until blended. Change to a dough hook and knead for 2 minutes on low speed, then 2 more minutes on medium speed. Please note that this is a sticky dough and you must have a powerful mixer. The dough should be moist and elastic.

Place the dough in an oiled bowl, cover tightly with plastic wrap and let rise in a warm room until doubled in size, about 2 hours. Punch the dough down and cut in half on a lightly floured surface. Shape each piece into a round loaf and place on a buttered or parchment paper-lined baking sheet. Cover with a semi-damp towel and let rise in a warm room for about 1 1/2 hours or until doubled in bulk. Bake in a 450-degree oven for 15 minutes. Reduce the heat to 375 degrees and bake loaves for another 25 minutes. Cool on a rack before serving.

Capirotada a la Celina

Every region of Mexico has its own version of this syrup-coated, bread pudding-like dessert. It is traditionally served during Lent. Kitchens in northern Mexico add cheese to the dish. This recipe was shared with me by longtime friend Celina Rios Mullan. I met Celina and her husband, renowned artist G.E. Mullan, when I was looking to acquire a painting of Saint Anthony of Padua as a gift for my mother. G.E. had been commissioned by the Archdiocese of San Antonio, Texas, to paint one for Pope John Paul II to commemorate his visit to the city, and I wanted one like it. Years later, our families are still friends. G.E. and Celina even attended the commencement exercises when I graduated from the Culinary Institute of America in New York. When writing down this recipe for me, Celina explained that it was as close to her father's as she could get.
¡Buen Provecho!

Mix the brown sugar, water, cinnamon sticks and cloves in a large sauce pot. Bring to a boil, reduce heat and simmer.

Add the raisins, apples and brandy. Simmer for 15 minutes. Remove the cinnamon sticks and cloves. While this is cooling, toss the bread with the melted butter in a large bowl. Place on a sheet pan and bake in a 375-degree oven for about 15 minutes or until toasted.

Butter a 13×9-inch pan. Layer 1/2 of the toasted bread crumbs followed by 1/2 of the liquid, 1/2 of the pecans, and 1/2 of the cheese. Repeat. Place a cinnamon stick standing straight up in the center. Cover with foil, forming a tent. Bake in a 300-degree oven for 1 hour. Turn the heat off and let rest in the oven for at least another hour before serving.

Ingredients

2 cups packed brown sugar
5 cups water
6 cinnamon sticks
4 whole cloves
1 cup raisins
2 apples, chopped
2 tablespoons brandy
20 to 24 ounces challah or egg bread, cubed
1/2 cup (1 stick) butter, melted
1 cup chopped pecans
1 pound sharp Cheddar cheese, shredded

Chocolate Terrine

SERVES TEN

You may remember me mentioning that chocolate does nothing for me. This Chocolate Terrine, which comes from the kitchens of Bayona in New Orleans, Louisiana, is an exception. While working the dessert station there, I always hoped that a slice would be messed up while being cut so that I could enjoy it. Unfortunately, it rarely happened, so I had to content myself with the end pieces that were not presentable. This dessert is especially good served with crème anglaise and fresh strawberries or raspberries.

Ingredients

1 1/2 cups half-and-half
1 ounce heavy cream
6 ounces butter
9 ounces bittersweet chocolate
3 ounces unsweetened chocolate
3/4 cup sugar
3 tablespoons cocoa powder
6 eggs
3 tablespoons brandy
Confectioners' sugar
1 (7-ounce) package almond paste
2 ounces butter
1 ounce corn syrup
6 ounces bittersweet chocolate

Heat the half-and-half, cream and 6 ounces butter in a large sauce pan. Add 9 ounces bittersweet chocolate and the unsweetened chocolate and melt. Mix the sugar and cocoa powder together and add, stirring until there are no lumps.

Mix the eggs and brandy together and add. Pour into a terrine mold that has been buttered and lined as smoothly as possible with foil. Bake in a water bath for 40 minutes. Cool completely before unmolding. Chill in the refrigerator until needed.

Using some confectioners' sugar to dust your surface and rolling pin, roll the almond paste into a thin layer that is large enough to cover the top and the 2 long sides of the unmolded terrine, bottom side up. Place the terrine on a rack, over a pan. Return to the refrigerator.

Melt 2 ounces butter with the corn syrup. Add 6 ounces bittersweet chocolate and mix well until melted. Glaze the terrine with this mixture. Return to the refrigerator. Keep cold until ready to serve.

To serve, use a very sharp knife dipped in hot water and cut slices about 3/4 inch thick. For an extra special treat, serve atop crème anglaise with fresh berries.

Peach Blueberry Bread Pudding with Lime Curd

The secret behind this bread pudding is the cheese Danish used for the "bread" part of the pudding. It makes for a great departure from the traditional stale bread typically reserved for this dessert. I made this for a press party one time and I don't think any pictures were taken or questions asked—they were all too busy enjoying this delectable treat.

SERVES ABOUT TWELVE

Peach Blueberry Bread Pudding

Soak the blueberries n the Triple Sec for 1 hour and then microwave the mix on High for 2 minutes. Drain the liquid and sip on it while finishing the recipe! Set the blueberries aside.

Place the cubed cheese Danish in a 2-quart oval baking dish (preferably). Add the blueberries, crushed peaches and their juice and toss together.

Pour the cream and the vanilla into a small heavy-bottomed pot. Whisk together the sugar and the egg yolks and combine them with the cream mixture. Heat over medium heat, stirring occasionally, until warm to the touch. Pour over the Danish mixture and set aside for 30 minutes, covered with foil. Meanwhile, preheat the oven to 350 degrees.

Place the baking dish in the oven and bake, covered, for 40 minutes. Uncover and bake for another 15 to 20 minutes or until the pudding is firm but not dry.

After the pudding has rested out of the oven for at least an hour, pour the entire recipe of Lime Curd over it.

Lime Curd

In a sauce pot, combine the lime juice and sugar. Bring to a rolling boil. Boil for 3 minutes.

In a separate bowl, whisk together the egg yolks. Slowly whisk in 1 tablespoon of the hot juice mixture. Repeat 3 more times, being careful not to cook the egg yolks.

Quickly whisk the egg yolk mixture back into the remainder of the juice and sugar. Stirring constantly, cook over low heat until it begins to thicken. Remove from the heat.

Place in a bowl and stir in the butter until blended. Cover and place in the refrigerator for 2 to 3 hours or until set.

Peach Blueberry Bread Pudding

3/4 cup dried blueberries

1/3 cup Triple Sec

1 3/4 pounds cheese Danish, cut into 1-inch cubes

1 (23 1/2-ounce) can peaches in juice, crushed

1 pint heavy cream

1 teaspoon vanilla extract

1/2 cup sugar

8 egg yolks

Lime Curd

Lime Curd

2/3 cup fresh lime juice

2/3 cup sugar

6 egg yolks

1/2 cup (1 stick) butter, cut into pieces

Thank you...

Mom for your patience while using your kitchen as my test kitchen and for your editorial pass over of this book before it was submitted. **Dad** for always being there for me and for your financial advice. **Tommy** for being my main bowl-licker and for the high ranks you always award my food. **Elma Salinas Chapa Henry (a.k.a. Granny)** for your love, your humor, your attitude, and your common sense. You guided me through your kitchen and taught me all that you knew along with what Edward (my Grandfather) had shown you. **Alicia Simona Flores de Flores (a.k.a. Uelita)** for taking the time out of your hectic life and showing me your knowledge of the Mexican kitchen. Uelito (Daniel) was the head of the household, but you were the neck that held it up and made it turn. **Rosa Alaniz** for helping to take care of me and teaching me some basic skills of Mexican cooking. **Ray & Helen Comer**. Tio, you taught me about cocktail hour (for which I am eternally grateful!) and Tia, you introduced me to Greek food and the concept of having an overflowing refrigerator and pantry anytime guests were present. **Chrisylaine Tarrillion** for sharing with me some of Tia's recipes and for being my "link" to her. I guess our love for her makes us family. **Fernando Flores** for all of your computer and technical help. **Susan Spicer** for your friendship, culinary guidance, and for always being there whenever I ask—last minute or not!

Regina & Ron Keever for opening the door to Bayona for me. **Regina Mosel** for all of your feedback while sampling my test recipes and help in answering my liquor questions. **The Sisters of the Sacred Heart of Jesus of St. Jacut** for providing me with a foundation for life, friendship, and prayers.

The Reverends Patrick O'Shea & John Finn for your spiritual support and for providing an outlet for all of my test batches to be enjoyed.

Brother Cletus Behlman for providing all the great artwork in this book—ahead of schedule and under budget. **Sue Leone** for your help in recipe development, your friendship, and your excitement over this book. **Joe Saglimbeni** for introducing me to Sue and for supporting me and my business since the beginning. **Employees at Saglimbeni's** for your help in answering my wine and spirits questions. **Jan Green,** *my* "official" chef.

Donna Delire, my high school algebra teacher at Central Catholic Marianist College Preparatory. I never would have made it through college, culinary math, or this book without all the math skills that you taught me. **The Culinary Institute of America, its faculty, staff, & administration** for an incredible culinary foundation and two of the best years of my life. **G.E. and Celina Rios Mullan** for being two of the first mentors in my culinary career and a constant sounding board. **Lynn Nicklo** for holding my hand and guiding me through each and every step of the food processing and manufacturing world. Without you and the Hösgood's team my company would not be where it is today. **Terry Bohr** of Marquee Foods in Houston, Texas, for your patience, knowledge, and dedication to quality when it comes to producing my gourmet product line. I've learned a lot from you. **Sandra Roy** for your quick copyediting of my written voice. **John Ash, Bruce Auden, David Garrido, Anne Kearney, Matt Martinez, & Pat Mozersky** for your kind words and high praises. **Family & Friends** (not mentioned by name) who have supported me throughout my culinary journey. **God** . . . for the talents and gifts you have bestowed upon me that have made it possible to write this book.

Biographies

MICHAEL H. FLORES

Chef Michael H. Flores' roots are based in classical cuisine and run as deep as the simmering stockpots of his grandmothers' kitchens. He has a degree and honors from the Culinary Institute of America and interned with acclaimed Chef Susan Spicer. Currently, Chef Flores creates and produces his own line of gourmet products appropriately called "Chef Michael H. Flores." He has had the honor of cooking at the renowned James Beard House in New York City, and awards received include the coveted "People's Choice Award" at the nationally acclaimed Texas Hill Country Wine & Food Festival.

Hailed as "a San Antonio phenomenon" and "whiz-kid chef" by the media, the unique culinary creations of Flores rely upon traditional methods of classical cuisine while they incorporate ingredients from diverse cultures. In this multi-cultural diversity, he explores the richness of flavors, aromas, and presentation, a culinary journey that reflects his appreciation of peoples and their lives mirrored in their foods.

Chef Michael H. Flores continues to reside in San Antonio, Texas, with his brother and business partner, Tommy. San Antonio is home base for Chef Flores' company, Mis En Place L.L.C. There, he continues to be involved in developing and marketing more products for his gourmet product line. Visit him on the world wide web at chefmichael.com.

SUSAN SPICER

Susan Spicer began her cooking career in New Orleans as an apprentice to Chef Daniel Bonnot at the Louis XVI Restaurant in 1979. In 1986, she opened the tiny Bistro at Maison de Ville in the Hotel Maison de Ville, also in New Orleans. Four years later, she opened Bayona in a beautiful, 200-year-old cottage in the French Quarter. With solid support from local diners and critics, Bayona soon earned national attention and has been featured in numerous publications from *Food & Wine* and *Food Arts* to *Travel and Leisure*, *Bon Appétit*, *The New York Times*, and more. Susan has been guest chef at The James Beard House, The Oriental Hotel in Bangkok, the Lanesborough in London, Cunard and Crystal Cruise Lines, as well as appeared on local and national television. In May 1993, she was the recipient of the James Beard Award for Best Chef of the Southeast and, in 1995, was chosen for the Mondavi Culinary Excellence Award.

Chef Spicer's restaurant, Bayona, has been featured as one of *Restaurants and Institutions'* Ivy Award Winners, as well as having been named to *Nation's Restaurant News'* Fine Dining Hall of Fame. Bayona has also been included in the "Top Five Restaurants in New Orleans" in *Gourmet's* Readers' Poll. While visiting New Orleans, Louisiana, look for Susan Spicer in the kitchens of Bayona, Herbsaint, or Cobalt.

BRO. CLETUS BEHLMANN

Bro. Cletus Behlmann, S.M. (Marianist), a well-known San Antonio artist, taught for 19 years before settling in San Antonio as the operator of St. Mary's University Gallery, Studio, and Art Center. Thanks to his artistic inventiveness, the Center reflects art and conveys beauty. Bro. Cletus has a drive that fires both his creative imagination and productivity. He works in a variety of media: metal, acrylic, watercolor, batik, pastel, stained glass, ceramics, handmade paper, linoleum prints, collage, and others. He has been called "shockingly productive." Although his themes range from religious to folk art to abstract, the overall leitmotif of his work is in "celebration of life," from the wonders of nature to the wonders of God's Redemption.

Bro. Cletus also loves to combine travel with his painting. He has traveled and painted in much of the United States, Japan, China, Hong Kong, Taipei, Bangkok, most of the European countries, and much of Central America. Bro. Cletus states, "Combining travel and painting is one of my favorite things. Although most of my waking hours are devoted to art, I don't think of it as a job . . . it is something I love to do. I think it is my passion in life and for that I am eternally grateful."

For more information, visit his web site at www.brothercletus.com.

My Family

Helen Comer (Tia), 49, 63, 130, 176
Ray Comer (Tio), 49, 63, 176
Cousin Eddie, 36
Alicia Simona Flores de Flores (Uelita), 11, 19, 136, 150, 161, 176
Apolonio (Nono) Flores (Dad), 51, 64, 74, 139, 153, 155, 156, 176
Daniel Flores, Sr. (Uelito), 176
Fernando Flores (Uncle), 159, 176
Mary Helen Flores (Mom), 10, 11, 19, 44, 64, 112, 139, 141, 153, 156, 157,
159, 163, 167, 173, 176
Thomas J. Flores (my brother), 44, 52, 78, 92, 153, 154, 156, 167, 170, 171, 176
Mague Flores-Nutt (Aunt), 12, 74
Elma Salinas Chapa Henry (Granny), 11, 19, 144, 150, 161, 163, 176
Cousin Marci, 14
Dennis "Brick" Pennock (Cousin), 15
Rich Pennock (Cousin) and Carmela, 79

My Friends

Rosa Alaniz (housekeeper), 92, 139, 142, 176
Jo Ann Andera, 139
John Ash, 177
Bruce Auden, 177
Brother Cletus Behlman, 176
Terry Bohr, 177
Julia Child, 29, 99
Mrs. Eileen (John) Daniels, 53
Donna Delire, 177
Reverend John Finn, 176
Sr. Alice Garcia, 133
David Garrido, 177
Jan Green, 177
Cynthia Guido, 145, 149
Sylvia Herrera, 13
Spero Kannavos, 35, 117
Anne Kearney, 177
Regina Keever, 16, 176
Ron Keever, 176
Lance Leaming, 16
Sue Leone, 67, 78, 79, 162, 164, 176
Matt Martinez, 154, 177
Regina Mosel, 176

Pat Mozersky, 123, 177
Celina Rios Mullan, 15, 101, 166, 173, 177
G. E. Mullan, 101, 173, 177
Joe Nicklo, 52
Lynn Nicklo, 19, 52, 177
Reverend Patrick O'Shea, 83, 176
People's Choice Award, 89, 118
Sisters of the Sacred Heart of Jesus
of St. Jacut, 13, 176
Susan Spicer, 8, 9, 16, 17, 50, 110,
137, 159, 176
Sr. Philomena Rios, 15, 167
Sr. Cecilia Rodriguez, 167
Sandra Roy, 177
Joe Saglimbeni, 67, 73, 176
April Smith, 56
Ed Snider, 43, 60
Patsy Swendson, 95
Sr. Juana Villescas, 167
Brother Ed Violet, 132
Chrisylaine Tarrillion, 176
Sr. Ernestine Trujillo, 13, 159

My Food

Jalapeño Chiles

Beef Vegetable Soup, 64
Calabacita, 150
Chilaquiles de Nopal y Camarones
  con Huevos, 151
Cilantro Slaw, 56
Fried Blue Corn Dusted Catfish with
  Avocado-Preserved Lemon
  Salsa, 108
Gorgonzola Pumpkin Seed Salsa, 123
Migas, 156
Mini Crayfish Tostadas with
  Avocado & Corn, 103
Rosa's Chile Cheese Potatoes, 92
Tilapia Veracruz Style, 117
Tomato Cheese Sauce, 143
Tortilla Salad, 112
Vermicelli Soup (Sopa de Fideo), 62

Lamb

Greek Lamb Chops, 127
Hoisin-Glazed Lamb, 127
Mediterranean Nachos, 29

Lentils

Lentil Salad, 39
Red Snapper Atop Green Lentils
  with Dijon Vinaigrette, 116

Manchego

Cilantro Pesto, 28
Eggplant in Romesco Sauce with
  Manchego Cheese, 89
New Potatoes with Escargot,
  Cilantro Pesto & Brie, 28
Pepita Crusted Chicken Breasts Stuffed
  with Chorizo & Manchego Cheese
  with a Roasted Red Pepper
  Sauce, 131

Marinades

Beef Kebabs, 126
Cumin Vinaigrette, 58
Greek Lamb Chops, 127
Hoisin Marinade, 127
Stuffed Ancho Chiles, 145

Masa Harina

Fried Oysters, 54
Sweet Corn Cakes Topped with Salad of
  Shrimp, Avocado & Cubed Queso
  Blanco with Tomatillo Vinaigrette, 107
Tamales Chiapanecos, 149

Meatless Entrées

Gâteau d'Aubergines on a Lentil Salad
  with Feta Cheese & Sundried
  Tomato Aïoli, 38
Garlic-Vegetable Penne, 80
Pasta alla Puttanesca, 71

Monterey Jack

Chilaquiles, 155
Enchiladas in Ancho Chiles Topped
  with Tomato Cheese Sauce, 142
Migas, 156

Mozzarella

Enchiladas in Ancho Chiles Topped
  with Tomato Cheese Sauce, 142
Rosa's Chile Cheese Potatoes, 92

Mushrooms

Apples Stuffed with Mushrooms, 95
Artichokes, Mushrooms & Peppers
  with Cumin, 35
Gâteau d'Aubergines on a Lentil Salad
  with Feta Cheese & Sundried
  Tomato Aïoli, 38
Mini Ravioli with Sundried Tomato Pesto
  Atop Grilled Portobello Mushrooms, 42
Mushroom Brie Soup, 60
Mushroom Cream Gravy, 154
Mushroom-Rosemary Pesto, 77
Spaghetti with Sausage & Mushrooms, 80
Three-Cheese Soup with Basil Cream, 61

Nopal

Chilaquiles de Nopal y Camarones
  con Huevos, 151
Nopalitos con Camarones Seco, 144

Olives

Beef Stuffing, 136
Eggplant in Romesco Sauce with
  Manchego Cheese, 89
Eggplant Salad, 51
Greek Cucumber Salad, 49
Lentil Salad, 39
Mediterranean Nachos, 29
Mediterranean Torta, 34
Olive Butter, 124
Olive-Green Pepper Pesto, 77
Orzo Salad, 50
Pasta alla Puttanesca, 71
Tilapia Veracruz Style, 117
Ziti Pasta Salad, 52

Now that you have come to the end of my book—literally—and have thoroughly enjoyed every little morsel of it, may I suggest visiting my web site at:

www.chefmichael.com

There you will find my extensive, and might I add quite delicious, gourmet product line. Also on the web site are more recipes, gift ideas, personal stories (typically culinary based), and even a date book that lists cities I'm visiting along with scheduled events. You can contact me with any cooking question(s) you might have, or just to add your name to my mailing list. You can even purchase more of these cookbooks for all of your family and friends—personalized and signed by me!

If you are not "technically gifted," have no fear . . . I have a toll-free number that you can call. Or, if you'd prefer to be even more personal, you can write to me. All of the information is below.

I look forward to hearing from you. Until then, remember: eat to make yourself happy, all the while savoring every bite of life.

—Michael

Chef Michael H. Flores
Mis En Place, L.L.C.
Post Office Box 700882
San Antonio, Texas 78270
1-210-545-CHEF or 1-888-798-CHEF
1-494-0853 (facsimile)
www.chefmichael.com